John H. Kampmann

Master
Builder

John H. Kampmann

Master Builder

San Antonio's German Influence in the 19th Century

MAGGIE VALENTINE

BEAUFORT
BOOKS

Library of Congress Cataloging-in-Publication Data
Valentine, Maggie, 1949-
John H. Kampmann, master builder : San Antonio's German influence in the 19th century / by Maggie Valentine, PhD. -- First edition.
     pages cm
Includes bibliographical references and index.
ISBN 978-0-8253-0730-0 (hardcover : alk. paper)
1. Kampmann, John H., 1819-1885. 2. Architects--Texas--Biography. 3. German American architects--Biography. 4. San Antonio (Tex.)--Biography. I. Title.
NA737.K353V35 2014
720.92--dc23
[B]
                              2013036891

For inquiries about volume orders, please contact:
Beaufort Books
27 West 20th Street, Suite 1102
New York, NY 10011
sales@beaufortbooks.com

Published in the United States by Beaufort Books
www.beaufortbooks.com

Distributed by Midpoint Trade Books
www.midpointtrade.com

Printed in the United States of America

Interior design by Neuwirth & Associates, Inc.
Cover Design by Michael Short

{ Contents }

{ Foreword }

To say that Maggie Valentine's biography of Johann Hermann Kampmann has been long awaited is no mere cliché. Her meticulously documented work will be referenced by generations of historians and will encourage additional research into the myriad facets of his life. My wait began four decades ago in the course of a quest to identify the architectural legacy of the English-born architect Alfred Giles in Texas and Mexico. Upon Giles' arrival in San Antonio in 1873, he obtained employment in the office of master builder John Kampmann from whom he learned to utilize skillfully local building materials, especially stone. He worked for Kampmann for three years before establishing his own firm but the two would continue their collaborations until Kampmann's death in 1885.

Kampmann was an all-around man who left his imprint on virtually every aspect of San Antonio's urbanization process, yet all efforts through the years to locate documents providing evidence of his contributions had failed. All manner of information had been scattered among branches of his family down through the generations. These archives were carefully preserved by the maternal branch of the Kampmann family, which is cause for celebration now that the story is coming together in a timely way.

The long overdue re-emergence of the Kampmann story should encourage scholars to pursue other untold stories of the German-Texas connection. One spinoff already at work concerns German-born John Fries who moved to Texas in 1846 and to San Antonio in 1847—one year before Kampmann's arrival. Early on, Fries partnered with Kampmann as well as being competitive for jobs. Their formal relationship was dissolved but they continued to work together through the 1850s.

Until the not so distant past, families such as the Kampmanns did not have access to archives in which to do research or as a depository for historical documents—certainly not in Texas. There has also been an increase in the numbers of students in university graduate programs pursuing research topics under the tutelage of scholars such as Dr. Valentine. That these documents did not end up in a bonfire— as has often been the case— is additional cause for celebration.

Mary Carolyn Hollers George
Author *Alfred Giles: An English Architect in Texas and Mexico*
(Trinity University Press, 1972)

{ Acknowledgments }

This book started as a group project in my graduate Research Methods in Architecture class. My students did such good work that I felt it my duty to complete it. I am grateful to them (Brian Bienek, Chris Fincke, Raul Garcia, Rebecca Greathouse, Elizabeth Dobie Haynes, Brianna Janek, David Matiella, Whitney Mida, Javier Ramos, Jason Rodriguez, José Rosales, Lorraine Treviño, Amy Unger, Lauren Vasek, and Patricia Veliz) and to all my students who continue to teach and inspire me. Thanks to those who supported the project, including my colleagues in the College of Architecture, and the University of Texas at San Antonio for awarding me a Faculty Development Leave to work on it.

Thank you to a special group of people who read portions of the manuscript in progress and kept me from going too far astray. They shared their time, insights, anecdotes, and photographs with me: Judith Carrington, Juanita Herff Chipman, Eric Kampmann, Marlene Richardson, Kenneth Bonnet, George Kampmann, Mary Carolyn Hollers George, Mark Fries, Sara Kennedy, and Garland Lasater.

Thank you to the archivists and librarians who helped me locate images and information, especially Tom Shelton at UTSA Special Collections, the staff of the Texana Room at the San Antonio Public Library, and Beth Standifird at the San Antonio Conservation Society.

Thank you to the staff at Beaufort Books who showed great patience, including Megan Trank, Michael Short, Sarah Lucie, and Felicia Minerva. My family and friends encouraged me and kept me laughing, especially Richard Tangum, Craig Blount, and Joanna Valentine.

John H. Kampmann

Master
Builder

Introduction

————◖•●•◗————

John H. Kampmann (1819–1885) was an imposing force during his lifetime but is today relatively unknown in his adopted city of San Antonio. A large body of work is associated with his career as builder, contractor, and civic leader. Although much of it no longer survives, it was part of what changed the face of the city from mostly Spanish to partially German. An exploration of Kampmann's work also addresses what it meant to be an architect before the term acquired its legal definition as a profession.

German immigrant Johann Hermann Kampmann, a practicing craftsman trained in architecture in Germany, arrived in San Antonio in 1848. He became a builder, construction supervisor, and materials supplier in Texas. By the 1870s, he was listed as an architect in his paid ads as well as in the city directories. He was always a real estate investor and trader, and over the course of three and a half decades, he built up a large portfolio, probably the largest in the city, according to his obituary. Street signs still give testimony to his landholdings throughout the area. Over his thirty-five-year residency in the city, the newspapers touted him as "the first enterprising builder in San Antonio," "the busiest man in town," the largest employer and the third largest real estate owner in the city, and, at his death, as a "worthy citizen [...whose] loss [San Antonio] can little afford."

Family members saw him as a self-made man and the most important architect in what became the largest city in Texas. In his lifetime he was a stonemason, builder, soldier, factory owner, real estate magnate, politician, banker, businessman, patriarch, and millionaire. He was an entrepreneur who arrived in Texas at the right time, took advantage of the social network established by his fellow German immigrants, and became a booster and self-promoter who worked to build up his adopted hometown and become one of its leading citizens. In the process, he helped change the architectural face of the adobe Spanish village into a city of stone and mortar with a regional Texas German accent.

In 1850, San Antonio was the second largest city in the newly admitted state of Texas. The population was 3,488, with a density of ninety-seven persons per square mile. The thirty-six-square-mile city was still predominantly Spanish, with neighborhoods of Anglos, Irish, and, beginning in the 1840s, Germans. By the time Kampmann died thirty-five years later, the Spanish town had become a tri-cultural American city, and the United States had survived its greatest threat, the Civil War.

By 1890, five years after Kampmann's death, San Antonio was the largest city in Texas. It was still thirty-six square miles, but the population and density had increased 10.8 times to 37,673, and 1,046 persons per square mile. The city was filled with framed Anglo houses and sturdy German Hill Country limestone houses and churches. Prestigious educational institutions included the German-English School; clubs such as Casino Club and the Masonic Lodge dictated the social calendar. An effective trolley system begun in 1878 served downtown from the International and Great Northern (IGN) on the West Side, north to Alamo Heights. There were a number of banks, breweries, and skyscrapers downtown; the city had a metropolitan water company, as well as electricity and gas, and most of the streets were paved. John H. Kampmann was involved in most of these accomplishments and helped give San Antonio its distinctive profile; indeed, the San Antonio *Express News* in 1871 credited him with having built one-third of the city.

His clients included names still familiar in the city, including Menger, Halff, Steves, Hummel, Sweet, Eagar, Degen, Groos, and Oppenheimer, and his heirs are still known in the city and the region. But his buildings still speak the loudest about his accomplishments: the Dashiell (Fig Tree Restaurant), Steves, Eagar (HemisFair), and Sweet (University of the Incarnate Word) Houses; the German-English School; St. Joseph's Catholic and St. Mark's Episcopal Churches; and the Lone Star Brewery (San Antonio Museum of Art). They tell of life in San Antonio over the last 160 years, of evolution, adaptation, restoration, re-use, and, alas, some lost opportunities (Friedrich Groos House, Kampmann Building).

The organization of this book is both chronological and thematic. It traces Kampmann's development and contributions in San Antonio framed in terms of periods, which overlap in time. Chapter 1 investigates his life in Germany, although not much is known about the details; chapter 2 describes his arrival in Texas and San Antonio, and his early work with fellow German builder and architect John Fries. Chapter 3 focuses on his early independent practice and the expansion of the Texas German vernacular house as it developed in San Antonio. Chapter 4 chronicles Kampmann's role as an important player in the growing German American community in San Antonio, the source of most of his business, and his participation in the Civil War. Chapter 5 discusses the re-establishment of his career in San Antonio following the war; chapter 6 explores his involvement in the City of San Antonio as an entrepreneur and the creation of a public persona/benefactor; and chapter 7 analyzes his legacy and addresses the context of his work.

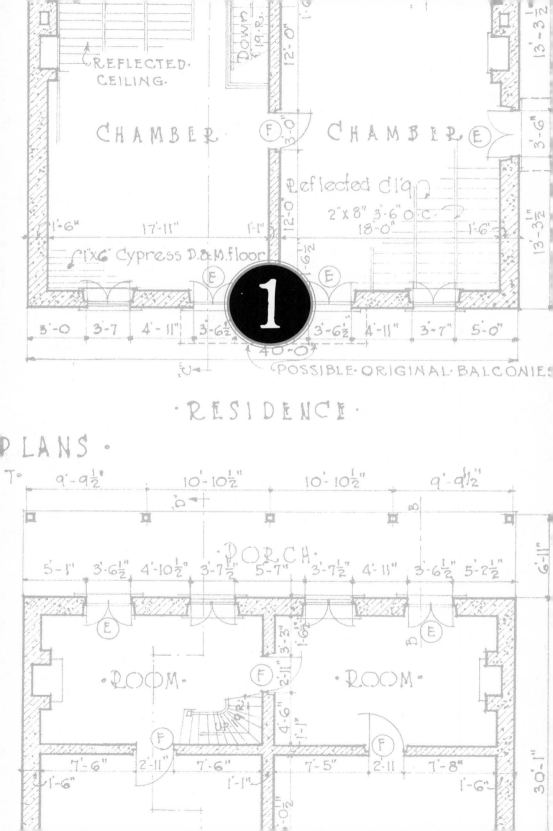

CHAMBER   CHAMBER

REFLECTED CEILING.

Down 19.R.

12'-0"

F (circled)   3'-0"   E (circled)

Reflected cl'g.

2"x 8" 3'-6 O C.

12'-0"

13'-3½"

3'-6"

13'-3½"

1'-6"   17'-11"   1'-1"   18'-0"   1'-6"

1"x 6" Cypress D. & M. floor

E (circled)   E (circled)

3'-0 | 3'-7 | 4'-11" | 3'-6½ | 3'-6½ | 4'-11" | 3'-7" | 5'-0"

40'-0"

POSSIBLE·ORIGINAL·BALCONIES

· R E S I D E N C E ·

P L A N S ·

9'-9½" | 10'-10½" | 10'-10½" | 9'-9½"

· P O R C H ·

5'-1" | 3'-6½" | 4'-10½" | 3'-7½" | 5'-7" | 3'-7½" | 4'-11" | 3'-6½" | 5'-2½"

6'-1"

E (circled)   E (circled)

· R O O M ·   · R O O M ·

F (circled)   3'-3"   2'-11"

F (circled)   4'-6"   F (circled)

UP 21 R.

30'-1"

7'-6" | 2'-11 | 7'-6" | 7'-5" | 2'-11 | 7'-8"

1'-6"   1'-1"   1'-6"

German Roots,
1819–1848

—◄)•●•(►—

I n 1819, Waltrop was a small rural town in the district of Vest Reckling-
hausen in North Rhine-Westphalia in Prussia. It was there on Christmas
Day that Elizabeth Fenniman Kampmann gave birth to a son, christened Johann Hermann [or Herrmann] Kampmann.

His father Peter worked as a farmer and died in 1833, when Johann was
fourteen years old. In 1833, fourteen-year-old German children would
have completed their education through the *Volksschule,* the common
school compulsory for German children beginning at age six or seven.
At this point, parents had to decide what route their children's education
would follow. Due to his father's death, Kampmann left his village for
Cologne, where he pursued a technical education in the building arts
and sought employment. For the next three years, he learned the trades
of locksmith, blacksmith, carpenter, mason, and stone-cutter, working
in the summer, and studying for three years at the Academy of Builders
during the winter.[1]

• • •

Architectural Education in Germany in the Nineteenth Century

Being an architect in nineteenth-century Germany carried with it some social standing, but no defined set of professional responsibilities. While the practice included building, engineering, artistry, and archaeology, it inherited little of the respect of those other professions. This was a different situation than in England or France, or even Germany in previous times, partially because Germany's historic roots were Gothic and Baroque rather than Classical, so that when Greco-Roman architecture became more dominant, Germany was not seen as an authoritative source.

Concurrently there was a shift in ideology regarding style. The Battle of the Styles in the nineteenth century was being won by the romantic view of medievalism in Germany, which historically never had much of a classical tradition. Classicism in Germany was interpreted as simplicity of form more than the details of the forms themselves. A.W.N. Pugin's arguments for the moral superiority of Christian architecture found expression, even if only superficially, in Prussian/German nationalism: architecture as patriotism and form trumping meaning. Thus religious buildings were seen as valid precedents for railway stations and public buildings.

There were three forms of education available to German students interested in an architectural career. Classically trained architects attended the *Akademie* and focused on the theoretical and artistic side of the profession, as opposed to the technical or practical aspects. But the leading German architects were more interested in building than educating, and the academies were in reality vocational schools aimed at honing students' craftsmanship. Karl Friedrich Schinkel, himself a classicist who became increasingly interested in Gothic Revival, recommended that future architects learn from workshops of *Meisterklasses*. These were professional offices similar to the ateliers where French students learned the practical side of building as apprentices. Lastly, the *Technische Hochschule* encouraged a technical rather than artistic education to train students for work in civil service or in engineering and shipbuilding.[2]

These three forms of professional education appeared to work independently of one another, and graduates from any one of them called themselves architects, whether they were artists, technicians, or civil servants. Whatever the title, the practice of architecture and construction was seen primarily as a craft. Kampmann attended the *Bauakademie* [Academy for Builders], where his education was in the craftsmanship and technical knowledge of building rather than theoretical foundations.[3]

After a mandatory two or three years in the Prussian Army in the late 1830s, Kampmann returned to Cologne and apprenticed as a stonemason on at least two major churches under the direction of Ernst Friedrich Zwirner and spent four years as chief architect and construction supervisor for Count von Fürstenberg while still in his twenties.[4]

Little is known about Kampmann's specific duties and contributions or those of his master teachers. He learned construction from a contractor named Heiden, with whom he worked on several projects, including the Church of St. Apollinaris in Remagen (1839–43), and he was employed as a stonemason on the Cologne Cathedral (*Kölner Dom*) (1842–61) in its early stages. Both of these churches were completed by Ernst Friedrich Zwirner (1802–1861), an architect who had studied in Berlin under the leading Prussian architect Karl Friedrich Schinkel and come to Cologne in 1833. But unlike Schinkel, who was modernizing classicism through abstraction, Zwirner, as his biographer pointed out, "insisted on faithful adherence to High Gothic details."[5] Over Zwirner's lifetime, he trained scores of stonemasons. The two churches that Kampmann worked on under Zwirner are, in fact, considered the most important religious buildings that demonstrate the German Neo-Gothic style.[6]

The Church of St. Apollinaris [*Apollinariskirche*] in Remagen, Germany, built on the Apollinaris Mountain along the Rhine, still serves as a pilgrimage church housing relics of St. Apollinaris, first Bishop of Ravenna, ca. 200.[7] In 1838, Count Franz Egon von Fürstenberg-Stammheim came into possession of the church and the monastery. He planned to renovate the pilgrimage site and be buried in the chapel crypt with the relics. When the old foundation was discovered to be insufficient, von Furstenberg hosted a competition for the design of a new

Fig 1. St. Apollinaris in Remagen overlooking the Rhine, ca. 1900 [Library of Congress]

church, which Zwirner won, utilizing the thirteenth-century medieval drawings planned for the cathedral.

The detailing on the new façade at Remagen resembled that of the Cologne cathedral. This may be seen best in the cast-iron filigree spires of the west towers overlooking the Rhine. The use of cast iron instead of masonry gave the church a shimmering effect when reflected in the water. The main body of the church itself is of quarry slate stone with an ashlar facing of volcanic rock called tuff, similar to Italian tufa. Much of the tracery as well as the eastern spires are yellow limestone. It is logical to infer that this is the part of the building that Kampmann may have worked on, given his apprenticeship in stonemasonry, as well as his subsequent work in San Antonio on limestone houses and churches.

Zwirner worked with Karl Friedrich Schinkel on the plans for the Cologne cathedral just prior to Schinkel's death in 1841 at the age of sixty, and construction commenced the following year. The partially completed western towers, abandoned in the sixteenth century, were the inspiration for the Gothic Revival work. Recently rediscovered medieval drawings of the west façade of the original cathedral design begun in 1238 were used as the basis for completing the cathedral work.[8] Kampmann undoubtedly worked in Zwirner's revived *Dombaübutte*, a cathedral workshop used for medieval construction, refining his skills as a stonemason and learning about the art and science of architecture and construction, as well as the importance of attention to detail. Here he would have observed or participated in several aspects of building. His biographies credit him as construction supervisor at St. Apollinaris and with four years as the principal architect for Count Fürstenberg at Steinheim [sic]. This probably refers to the years spent on the pilgrimage church at Remagen, which consumed all of Fürstenberg's energies until his death in 1859, leaving little time to build anything

Fig 2. St. Apollinaris as reconstructed. The shorter western towers are done in cast iron, so they shimmer in the Rhine River, creating a picturesque approach. The taller eastern towers over the entrance are in stone. [Arcturus, 2005]

else. Kampmann left Europe in 1848, but Remagen was not consecrated until 1857, and the cathedral was completed much later.[9]

Kampmann left the Apollinaris project and the employment of Heiden, Zwirner, and von Fürstenberg when he was commissioned into the army in the late 1840s. He decided to leave Germany instead to avoid conscription. As he explained, "he was suspected of republican principles" by the king, and "his safety demanded immediate emigration."[10] Mid-nineteenth-century Germany saw a surge in emigration due to several factors, both *push* and *pull*.

The year 1848 was a crucial one in European politics. Political upheavals spread throughout the continent, some successful and some not. It was an uneasy time for all social classes, both winners and losers. The rebels shared a demand for liberal reforms, such as free speech, religious liberty, and educational reform, but disagreed as to how radical these changes should be. In most countries, the demands for political, social, and economic progress were met with violence and increased insecurity, at least in the short run. This insecurity was supplemented by the effects of the Industrial Revolution on craftsmen and workers, and by the inequities and pollution of factory life. German reformers saw their cause fail, while other nations succeeded.

Between Texas independence in 1836 and statehood in 1845, much ink was dedicated to the advantages in Texas for German settlers (often written by persons who had never set foot there) in an effort to establish a stronger Anglo-European presence in the Republic and later state of Texas. The political, economic, and social factors in Europe created a favorable audience for such literature and spurred the organization of the *Mainzer Adelsverein at Briebach am Rhein* and other organizations that encouraged emigration.[11] The failed 1848 Revolution created a political atmosphere of unrest with loyalties being questioned on both sides, including many who were escaping repercussions of military conscription and service. In addition to political discontent, social and economic factors were at play. Overpopulation meant rising unemployment and social costs, accompanied by increased taxation, so the need for new markets and the promises of cheap land and better opportunities enticed thousands of Germans to set sail for America.[12]

Which of these motivations spurred Kampmann's voyage is unclear; perhaps it was a combination of factors. With von Fürstenberg's help, he was granted a furlough to go to England, and from there he sailed to America in 1848 aboard the *Charlemagne*, with some of the Forty-Eighters, veterans of the failed revolution.[13] "He would, if he had remained in Germany," he said in his 1880 autobiographical statement, "have taken a high rank as architect and builder."[14] Instead the ship's manifest identified his occupation as "mason," listing his baggage as two chests.[15] Kampmann, age twenty-seven, landed in New Orleans May 30, 1848, describing himself as "poor in purse but proud and determined in spirit."[16] He then sailed to Galveston and traveled north to New Braunfels, where there was a growing German settlement.[17] While there, he lost what little money he had in a bad loan to a friend and found few prospects for work. After three months in the tightly knit German community, he

Fig 3. J. H. Kampmann as a dapper young architect about the time he left for America [from a Daguerreotype, courtesy of Judith Carrington]

Fig 4. Caroline Bonnet, 1840s in Frankfurt [courtesy of Juanita Herff Chipman]

decided to try his luck in the more urban San Antonio, which was also beginning to feel the impact of German immigration.

Three years earlier, Caroline Jacobine Bonnet (1830–1914) had arrived in America with her parents, Philip Daniel (1800–1883) and Anna Maria (1805–1884), and four surviving brothers, Johann Carl (John Charles 1828–1893), Johann Peter (Peter 1833–1863), Heinrich Daniel (Henry Daniel 1835–1926), and Johann Andreas (John Andrew 1838–1917).[18] They were also German emigrants who left Charlottenberg in Nassau, Hesse, in pursuit of greater cultural and religious freedom and came to America via Holland as members of the Meusebach Colony when Caroline was fifteen years old (see figure 4). After landing in Galveston aboard the *Harriet Lane*, they made their way to New Braunfels by ox team, and after a short time moved to San Antonio. Their first night in the city was spent camping on the grounds adjacent to the Alamo, where the bandstand was later built in the Plaza and across the street from what was to become the site of the Menger Hotel, built and eventually owned by Kampmann. The Bonnet family then moved into an adobe hut with a mud roof on the site of the Menger, where Indian raids occasionally interrupted their lives. Caroline's father bought teams of oxen and worked in carting as well as stock raising.

Carting, also referred to as hauling, was an important industry in mid-nineteenth-century Texas, on both a local and a regional level. Given the expanse of Texas, the proximity to Mexico, the threat of Indians, and the emergence of new towns and villages, as well as the growth of existing towns, pre-railroad trade depended on carts pulled by oxen to move goods inland from ships, within and between settlements, and across borders.

Many successful merchants and bankers got their start in long-distance hauling. It was an accessible business and much in demand.[19]

German immigrants began moving into San Antonio in large numbers in the late 1840s and early '50s. In 1841, the German population in Texas was estimated to be ten thousand—equal to nearly 10% of those moving to Texas from the United States.[20] By 1856, Germans constituted one-fifth of the white population in Texas.[21] By 1904, San Antonio's population was sixty thousand, one-third of whom were German.[22] Over this half century, the face of San Antonio changed from a predominantly Hispanic settlement to a uniquely Texan combination of a vernacular Hispanic-, German-, and English-American city.

The urban community that Kampmann, the Bonnets, and the sudden influx of German émigrés found at mid-century was Mexican Spanish. San Antonio was built around three plazas instead of the usual one—a derivation of the colonial Laws of the Indies—as the town began as a union of all three types of Spanish settlements: religious (*Plaza de Valero*/Alamo Plaza), *presidio* (*Plaza de Armas*/Military Plaza), and *pueblo* (*Plaza de las Islas*/Main Plaza). The building types and locations, the urban grid street pattern dictated by the plaza, and farmlands in long strips near the missions all followed customs specified by tradition and codified by Phillip II in 1573.

Except for the missions and the church, most buildings were single-story *jacales* and adobe structures. The *jacal* was a small rectangular hut, born in rural Mexico, consisting of vertical wooden poles buried a few inches in the ground, similar to the French vernacular *poteau-en-terre* method. Horizontal sticks and branches were woven through the posts, forming a stable framework that could be plastered inside and outside with mud or lime mortar, creating a thick-walled insulated dwelling. The walls supported a gable roof set into the notched poles, covered with thatch and sporting an occasional cactus. The earthen floor completed the single-room home, which typically had one door and two or three windows. Often, these were used as temporary houses until a more substantial adobe house could be built.

Adobe houses built of local mud or clay were widespread throughout the Middle East, northern Africa, and arid areas of the Americas. They are inexpensive, climate-friendly, and ecologically sound structures. When the Spanish discovered native Americans using hand-pressed adobe, they taught them to form the mud into bricks and dry them in the sun. What started as a one-room dwelling could easily be added on to to accommodate a growing family or fortune. The houses could be one or two rooms, or dozens, built facing the street and around interior courtyards. The doors were on the southern or eastern wall traditionally, and the thick-walled house provided protection from the sun as well as from enemies. The door could be barred from the inside and the entry (*zaguan*) and courtyards were large enough to accommodate a cart and animals.[23]

Indians, Mexicans, and *mestizos*, followed by transplanted Irish, French, German, American, and English San Antonians each added their particular ethnic adaptation of building types and styles, construction methods, and climatic responses into an evolving Texas vernacular tradition. By the turn of the century, the spoken, written, and architectural language and culture had become (and still is) multilingual. Much of this cultural transformation was due to J. H. Kampmann and his tight circle of German cohorts.

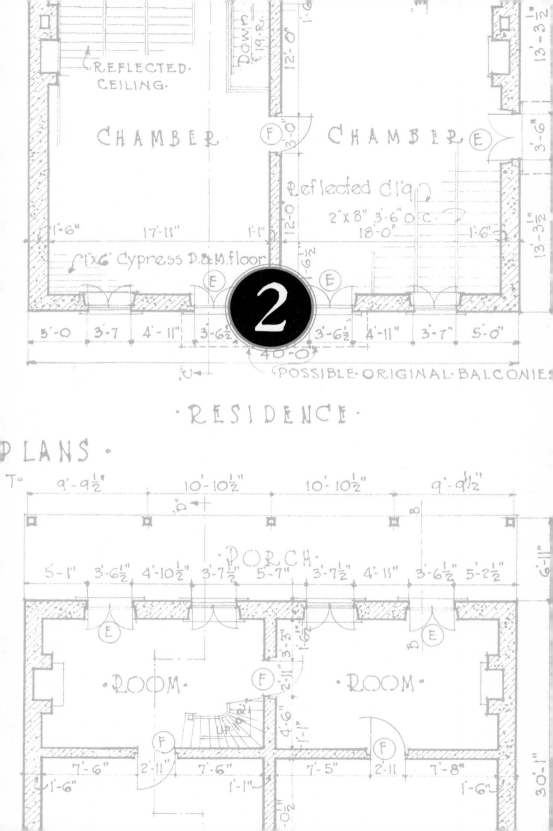

Gone to Texas
1848–1852

—————◗•●•◖—————

Johann Kampmann arrived in San Antonio in 1848 "practically in poverty," he said, "but [. . .] soon [. . .] on the high road to success."[1] He started with odd jobs and worked as a mechanic and stonemason for two years, trying to establish a practice as an architect and builder. Shortly after his arrival, he met another German émigré who was to become his mentor and partner: John Fries, who was almost an exact contemporary with a similar career path.

Johann M. Fries was born in Hannover, Germany, on October 13, 1817, making him one year older than Kampmann; he died circa 1880, predating Kampmann by five years.[2] The Fries family emigrated to Dayton, Ohio, when Johann was very young, and he arrived in San Antonio in about 1847, a year before Kampmann, establishing his reputation as a "builder-architect." While some accounts say he "received a good education and studied the profession" and "trained as an architect," his son Fred (City Clerk in San Antonio from 1905–1930) claimed he was not well educated, just gifted.[3] Texas historian Willard Robinson referred to Fries as "the city's first truly professional architect," but son Fred recalled, "My father used to work for a while, build a house or something, and then enjoy the money till he needed more. He often took long trips, between times."[4] This is further evidence of the lax definition of *architect*, a label that builders frequently claimed for themselves, as there existed no legal definition for *architect* at the time. In the 1860 federal census, Fries, age forty-two, identified himself as a "master mason." Neither Fries nor Kampmann left archived drawings or written records of their education or careers. They considered themselves to be in the construction businesses, which included designing when necessary.

One of Fries's first jobs in San Antonio was to repair the damaged façade of the Alamo for the U.S. Ordinance Department of the Army, which was leasing it from the Catholic Church and using it as a military storehouse. The mission church was unfinished at the time of the battle in 1836, and Fries, working with stonemason David Russi and Assistant Quartermaster Major Edwin Burr Babbitt, designed the now iconic shape on the front façade cornice in 1850.[5] The famous curved gable was to cover the end of the wooden roof built at the same time by the army. Kampmann began working with or for Fries in about 1848, but there is no record of his participation on the Alamo project; in fact, it is unlikely since Fries was working with Russi.[6]

Fries and Kampmann

Kampmann's early construction projects in San Antonio were houses near Alamo Plaza, including houses for Henry Bitter and for H. D. Stumberg. Not much is known about these projects, including the exact locations. Henry William Bitter, German immigrant, and his wife, Franciska, lived on the northwest corner of Villita and South Alamo Street in a two-story house built about 1850. This house was later used as a saloon, gambling house, and Mrs. Womble's boarding house, and was torn down in 1939. Or it may have been the Otto Bombach House at 231 S. Alamo, a limestone residence built by carpenter Bombach for his family in 1847, and the first two-story structure in San Antonio, which appears later as part of

Bitter's estate.[7] This house was used as a family residence, boarding house, saloon, desperados' hangout, and historical museum before it became the Little Rhein Steak House in 1967. Both Stumberg and Bitter owned many properties, frequently buying and selling, so the references may be to houses commissioned by them, not necessarily primary residences for their families. Herman Dietrich Stumberg arrived in San Antonio in 1839, establishing a food shop on Acéquia Street, which evolved into a very successful German bakery. Both Bitter and Stumberg became civic leaders in San Antonio, serving as aldermen, and Stumberg was an organizer of the mostly German Volunteer Fire Co. #2, which included Kampmann.[8]

It can be assumed that Fries and Kampmann were stonemasons for these structures; possibly Kampmann was an employee of Fries, who may have been acting as a contractor. According to an article in the San Antonio *Light* in September 1884, the Better [sic] House was still standing, but Stumberg's had been torn down for the Menger Hotel.[9] Both Fries and Kampmann were also accumulating land and social/business connections; newspaper clippings from the 1880s indicate further business transactions and social relationships among this small German immigrant group throughout their lives. Land deeds from the 1850s show that they were both amassing property in the city, together and independently.

Kampmann became Fries's business partner circa 1850. Their first joint construction projects were government buildings: the General Land Office Building in Austin; the Bastrop County Courthouse; and the municipal courthouse in San Antonio, known as the "Bat Cave." They also partnered on completion of the Hummel Building.

The General Land Office was established in 1837 to coordinate the scattered records of public and private land ownership in Texas and was housed in the first capitol building in Houston. When the capital was moved to Austin in 1839, the land office was in a log-frame building at Pine [7th] and Colorado, which burned down two years later.

The office moved again into headquarters built by Kampmann and Fries in 1851–52, located at the northwest corner of the capitol grounds on Colorado at Colorado and Peach [13th] Streets. It was described as a simple, square, single-story stone building with three rooms on either side of a corridor, its appearance "flat and uncouth."[10] Yet the drawing on the Texas General Land

Austin, TX – Colorado Street and Peach Street, 1851-1857

Fig 5. General Land Office, Austin 1851-57 [Texas General Land Office]

Office Web site depicts a solid two-story limestone building (see fig. 5).

Almost as soon as they moved in, they realized they needed a larger space, and by 1856, the office moved again into a larger fireproof German Romanesque building at 12th and Brazos Streets, designed by a draftsman working in the land office, Conrad G. Stremme. Nothing remains of Fries and Kampmann's first joint project. It was gone by 1873, when Augustus Koch's Bird's Eye map of Austin was done, which showed the new General Land Office Building.

Bastrop County, settled in 1829, conducted county business in a number of buildings that they quickly outgrew due to a rapidly increasing population. In 1851, $5,000 was earmarked for a new proper courthouse and jail.[11] In 1852, Mr. Fitzgerald was awarded fifty dollars for his plans for the construction of a new courthouse.[12] The building program was aided by the Texas State Legislature's relinquishing state taxes from Bastrop County for two years to aid in the construction.[13] The site was purchased in 1852, and the Odd Fellows laid the cornerstone containing coins from 1843–1851, for this, the third county courthouse in Bastrop. "In charge of building were contractors John Fried [sic] and Henry [sic] Kampmann."[14] The first payments to contractors "Frirs & Kampman [sic]" were made on February 18 and June 4, 1853.[15]

According to the *Bastrop County Commissioner's Minutes* Vol. A, quoted at length by Kenneth Kesselus, the building was spelled out in some detail by the commissioners, based on Fitzgerald's plans:

> To be built of good and well burnt brick 50 feet square from out-
> side of wall. Two stories high, the foundation to be of good solid

Fig 6. Bastrop Country Courthouse, 1854-83 [drawing by Gary Grief, 1987, courtesy of Kenneth Kesselus, 1987: 64]

stone; to commence three feet underground and terminate 2 feet above the same. [Both] stories to be 12 feet in the clair [clear]. The roof to be hipped. The lower outer on first story wall shall be 18 inches thick, the inner walls shall be 13 ½ inches thick.[16]

The description goes on to describe the measurements, placement, and materials for all windows and doors and finish details including paint colors, based on Fitzgerald's plans. The first floor was to have an entrance ten feet wide running through and leading to four rooms that measured seventeen by twenty-three feet. These rooms were to be used as prison cells and a dungeon, a jailor's room, one room for the county, and another for the district clerk.[17] The second floor contained the courtroom. Four windows fourteen by sixteen inches with twelve lights were aligned with windows on the upper floor, which measured twelve by fourteen inches with twelve lights. The windows were to be shuttered, outside doors paneled, and all timbers to be of clare [clear] hart [heart] pine. . . . The whole work to be done in workmanlike manner and to have two coats of white lead [paint] on wood work, except shingles, floors and joists. It is further ordered that the said house to be let to lowest bidder . . . [and] to be completed by the first of January 1853.[18]

There is some disagreement as to the courthouse's completion date. Bill Moore said the building was in use in early 1853, and Kesselus stated that by late May of 1853, "the foundation for the new jail and Court House (both in one building) ... (had been) laid and one of the dungeons for prisoners nearly completed."[19] Kesselus cited the *Bexar County Commissioners Courts Minutes* sale of "the old courthouse" and jail in 1855 to indicate that the job was completed in late 1854-early 1855.[20] However, according to the WPA (Works Progress Administration) Texas Historical Records Survey, "In 1855, apparently in expectation of soon occupying the new courthouse, the court contracted for 50 chairs of 'a Large Commodius Size to be made out of strong material with Raw hide Bottom and to be painted with two coats of Green or Blue Paint & Branded Ct or BC.'"[21] The report continued, "work on the courthouse was slow, and by 1857 it was apparent that the contractors would not complete their labors according to contract. In February the court appointed Thomas H. Mays and local merchant Henry Crocheran to have the building finished."[22]

The Bastrop courthouse served the county well until January 1883, when it was destroyed in a fire, and the present courthouse building designed by J. N. Preston and F. E. Ruffini replaced it on the same site. According to his 1894 biography, Kampmann lived in Bastrop while working on the courthouse, returning to San Antonio in 1852, before the building was completed.[23] Fries and Kampmann were clearly contractors for this building and probably stonemasons for the courthouse and the Land Office Building, as well as for their next project in San Antonio, the "Bat Cave." They started as rivals for this job, but ended as partners.

By this time, Kampmann had a family to support; Johann Kampmann and Caroline Bonnet married May 14, 1850. He was thirty-one years old and looking for work. She was a decade younger and eager to make a home and start a family. Their first two children, Carolina and Lena, died in infancy, but within the decade, she had given birth to three more children: Eda (also spelled Ida) (1855), Hermann (1857), and Gustav (1860). The family lived in a small house on N. Presa, which they shared with Caroline's younger brother, Johann Andreas (John Andrew), and five German boarders until they could afford to begin building their own house.[24] There was a strong German community in San Antonio in which newcomers were assisted by earlier arrivals.

In 1844, the San Antonio City Council and Mayor Edward Dwyer agreed that the city needed a new courthouse and jail. City council minutes called for the new joint structure to incorporate "rock and material from public buildings," but did not specify from which buildings.[25] Finally, on September 2, 1851, city council awarded a contract to Fries and Kampmann to build a temporary courthouse and jail, the third such facility in San Antonio after the *Cabildo* [city council building] and the *Casas Reales* [city hall].[26] In the meantime, the district and county courts had been meeting in private citizens' homes. The new two-story stone building was located on the north side of Military Plaza on the ruins of the old presidio barracks. It came to be known as the "Bat Cave" when the second-story became a favored roosting place for thousands of bats that had to be cleared out on a regular basis. Two long poles and a crosspiece of timber would be bumped against the canvas ceiling "just in case" so trials could proceed.[27] The pejorative term was used to refer to both the jail and the courthouse.

The jail contained four cells, two on each floor, with dirt floors on the ground level.[28] The adjacent two-story rock courthouse building served as a police station on the first floor and courtroom on the second floor. The main floor was for use by the county, while the city was relegated to the upper floor. In addition to county and city court proceedings, all municipal business was conducted here, from city council meetings to police court, even after 1872, when the county and city government functions were separated.

The jail sat behind and adjoined the courthouse, as seen in figure 7, surrounded by a high stone wall topped by broken glass and bottles cemented into the mortar. The sharp edges were to discourage prisoners from trying to scale the wall.[29] Retired policeman Ed Froboese recalled the building:

Fig 7. The walled jail and two-story "Bat Cave" courthouse on Military Plaza [Barnes, 1890: 110]

> I first joined the SA police force, back in 1886 [. . .] and I reported to [. . .] headquarters in the old "Bat Cave" [. . .] two years before they started work on the city hall. [. . .] It was a two-story building with a rock fence around it. On top of the fence were broken bottles placed in the concrete to prevent persons from climbing over or escaping from the inside. Prisoners were kept on the ground floor of the building and huge balls and chains were placed on their legs.[30]

Apparently, the entire facility proved deficient due to inadequate funding and poor materials. In the late 1850s, Bexar County announced plans for a new county jail. Both Fries and Kampmann submitted bids, but the contract was awarded to Fries. In 1858, City Council moved to the newly completed French Building. By 1859, the police force had relocated. These actions could also have been due to the extreme inflation and increasing crime experienced by the city as it approached a new government under the Confederacy and martial law.[31] When the new $35,000 jail on Cameron Street was completed in 1878, with a capacity for eighty-six prisoners, the "Bat Cave" was relegated to a police court containing city prisoners, as well as city police headquarters.[32] It was finally demolished sometime during construction of the new City Hall in the early 1890s.

1849–52 Charles and Caroline Hummel House
79 [270 W.] Commerce St.

Charles Hummel, and his wife, Caroline, arrived in San Antonio in 1847 and opened a successful business as a gunsmith, for which he had studied in Karlsruhe.[33] He was also a prominent member of the expanding German community and a founding member of Alamo Lodge No. 44 of the Ancient Free and Accepted Masons organized in San Antonio in 1847. He held several community leadership positions, including being elected alderman in San Antonio in 1850 and County Commissioner in 1860.[34] He had started building a house on W. Commerce in 1849 and wanted to expand it for his business, operating it with his adopted nephew as Charles Hummel and Son. Fries and Kampmann were asked to build the eastern addition. Construction was delayed due to widespread cholera and bad weather, but completed in 1852.[35]

The addition was a two-story structure built of stone, and one of the first buildings to change house construction in San Antonio from adobe to stone. Cecilia Steinfeldt described it as "an excellent example of competent building methods employed in early San Antonio. The dormer windows, the simple Classical pediment, and the lacy iron balcony with huge widows to floor level, show discerning taste and thoughtful planning for comfort and convenience."[36] "In 1852 the building was incomparably the finest in the city, and was looked on as a veritable palace."[37] It was described by contemporaries as "the finest and most imposing structure on Commerce St [. . . and] considered a magnificent building. There were but two or three two-story adobes, and the others, also of adobe, were but little better than Mexican Jacals. [sic]."[38]

Fig 8. Charles and Caroline Hummel Residence, 1852, adjoining Hummel & Son [courtesy of Judith Carrington]

The building's social significance was as important as its structural qualities. The Casino Association was organized and met here in the 1850s until it grew too large for the site.[39] It also served as a "clubhouse and the home of fashion and festivity," a beer garden (1852), the Buckhorn Saloon (1857), the Pacific Express company (1884), military headquarters (1856), a wine parlor, and eventually for "promiscuous purposes" (1895).[40] Decades later, when Commerce Street was being widened and the house was torn down, the San Antonio *Daily Express* described it as "the wonder of the city."[41] Charles Hummel and John Kampmann became lifelong friends, frequently visiting and even vacationing together; the Kampmann family knew him as "Papa Hummel."

The Fries and Kampmann partnership was dissolved circa 1852, but both men continued building and shaping the City of San Antonio independently and in tandem. Both continued to join German-American organizations and causes. Fries went on to build Greek Revival houses for John Vance (1857–59) and Nat Lewis (1850s), as well as the Menger Hotel (1858; see chapter 4), the State House in Austin (1854, 1856), and his most well-known building, the Greek Revival City Market House in San Antonio (1858; razed 1920s).[42] These were recognized as the most elegant dwellings in the state.[43] But by the early 1860s, Fries had left the city, perhaps due to his pro-Unionist loyalties, and was operating a sheep ranch in Gillespie County with his son.

Kampmann spent the next decades acquiring property, building a construction business, and getting involved in the German-American community as well as in San Antonio society and politics. He acquired limestone quarries on the outskirts of the city, hauling rocks by wagon to his rock yard at Ave E and 4th Street, where they were sawn, cut, and chiseled for his own projects as well as for other contractors.[44] When he wasn't hauling his own materials, he contracted his carting services with the City of San Antonio.[45] He was growing his portfolio, buying, developing, and selling properties. He began by purchasing lots from individuals and from the city, either personally or in partnership. By 1850, he held real estate worth five hundred dollars, and by 1860, twelve years after his arrival with "practically nothing," his total land holdings were reportedly worth fifty thousand dollars (the equivalent of $1.3 million today).[46]

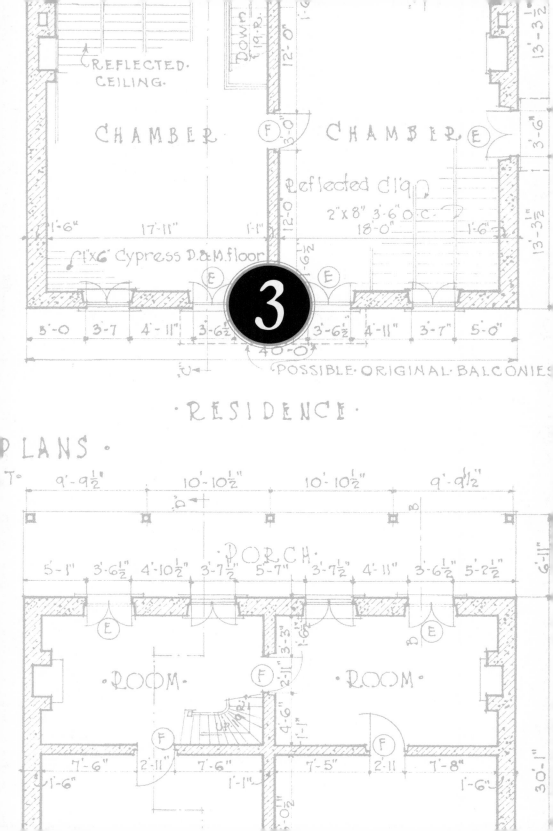

Texas–German
Vernacular
1854–1866

n October 1846, William A. McClintock wrote a letter to his parents describing his trip from Kentucky through Texas to Monterrey on his way to serve in the Mexican War. Passing through San Antonio, he noted that most houses still resembled fortresses, and "[w]ith the exception of two houses, of recent construction, on the American plan, not a house in the place, not even the govnors [sic], nor the chapel has any other than a dirt floor."[1]

In the 1850s, Kampmann found his first niche: variations of the simple vernacular German-Texas houses, combining the German hall and parlor house with the Texas dogtrot. These houses featured traditional German elements built with native Texas materials, coordinating masonry craftsmanship with wooden details. They were a regional vernacular version of Greek Revival, the first national American style, popular between 1820 and the Civil War. Carpenter's guides and pattern books made this style accessible to local builders as well as architects. Kampmann became a master of what Frederick Law Olmsted described as the epitome of San Antonio architecture in 1857:

The singularly composite character of the town is palpable at the entrance. For five minutes the houses were evidently German, of fresh square-cut blocks of creamy white limestone, mostly of a single story and humble proportions, but neat, and thoroughly roofed and finished. Some were furnished with the luxuries of little bow-windows, balconies or galleries.[2]

He could have been describing his first impressions of the Dashiell, des Mazieres, Sweet, or Eagar[3] Houses, built and perhaps designed by Kampmann in a vernacular style that addressed the climatic conditions of Texas. These simple limestone-block houses, called "rock houses" at the time, established his reputation in San Antonio and began to change the city's face from New World Spanish to Texan-German. Over the next several years, he perfected this form.

A main difference between the Spanish and German buildings was the choice of material. The former utilized thick adobe walls in the Southwestern tradition, which required minimal investment or trained labor and provided good insulation against both hot and cold weather. German builders relied on locally quarried limestone to create houses that resembled their cultural tradition and skills. "Soft rock" referred to the abundant mineral deposits found throughout the area. Easily quarried and worked, it could be cut into any shape with an ordinary hatchet or handsaw. When exposed to the air, it hardened, becoming strong and durable. These were often set using traditional Mexican masonry materials and techniques, creating a new Mexican-German-Texan hybrid.[4] Soft rock was generally used in smaller buildings, including houses; it was also used in making lime mortar. Equally plentiful was "hard rock,"—larger blocks of sedimentary rock hardened by exposure to the air and used in many public buildings. Cream-colored limestone became as symbolic of South Texas buildings as adobe had been, and they still exist side by side, amid the more modern technology of steel frames and glass curtain walls.

One of Kampmann's first soft-rock Greek Revival houses was a two-story German-style rock house on El Paseo [Houston Street] on the north bank of the San Antonio River, designed and built for Dr. Ferdinand and Mathilde Herff in 1853. Dr. Herff had his office in the substantial house, which also had a music room, where Mathilde taught piano and voice lessons; four bedrooms; and an indoor bathroom, still rare in those days. Behind the main house was another building containing the kitchen pantry and servant quarters, as well as a stable. The Herffs raised six sons (including Kampmann's son-in-law) in this house, which became a local landmark for the next six decades.[5] A handsome structure originally surrounded by cornfields and pastures, it was gradually dwarfed by the burgeoning downtown business district until the property was sold and the house razed in 1912, following Dr. Herff's death.

In 1854, Kampmann began building several other houses, including his own home, although it was not completed until the 1870s. The stucco-covered limestone des Mazieres House was a two-story variation of the same pattern, while the Sweet House was one of the best full-flowered examples of this new style that Kampmann stamped on San Antonio at mid-century. The other houses in this chapter follow variations of the same pattern. By the time he completed the Eagar House in 1870, the form was well known in the city as a recognizable type: the Texan–German vernacular Greek Revival.

1854 John H. and Caroline Kampmann House
311 Nacogdoches [demolished]

Kampmann began building a small "raised cottage" for his growing family on land he acquired that straddled the Alamo Acéquia Madre (Mother Ditch). The large lot was northeast of the Alamo in what was called "Irish Flats," because it was first settled by Irish settlers who arrived with the U.S. Army in 1846. In the 1850s, German settlers began moving into the neighborhood, which ran from Alamo Plaza north to 6th Street, and east-west from Avenue C [Broadway] to the Alamo Ditch. The family moved into the simple four-room hall and parlor limestone cottage in 1855, following the birth of daughter Eda. Limestone was found in abundance in San Antonio and the surrounding areas. Because it was easy to quarry

Fig 9. John and Caroline Kampmann House, 1850s [courtesy of Judith Carrington]

and work, it was a perfect building material. Construction on his own house went slowly, as he was building for other clients, and the house was not finished until after the Civil War. By that time Kampmann was a well-established businessman, and the completed house reflected his social standing and business success (see chapter 5).

Some of the floors were wood, some Spanish tile, some deep cement, and others of closely fitted flagstone, personally selected by Kampmann and hauled by mule team from the Helotes Creek. Originally built as a ranch house in open country that was considered far from the center of the city, which was then clustered around the old Spanish headquarters on the Military Plaza, the Kampmann House was a final stopping place for prairie schooners from Indianola, which brought money for payrolls, farm and lumber-mill hands, and supplies of every sort from Europe for the early settlers.[6]

Kampmann had already realized that he needed to expand his scope of work. He was a trained mason and a good craftsman, but now he began investing in the supply and delivery of materials as well as their application. He began leasing and eventually purchasing limestone quarries outside the city for use in his projects, as well as selling raw and finished materials to other builders. He owned enough real estate in the city that he could provide the site as well. He could draw plans based on repetitive patterns, so he advertised himself as an architect. He partnered with other people until it was not clear who contributed what skills to a project, but both could claim they *built* the house (as could the client). There was no clear legal definition of the word *architect* yet, so anyone in the building industry could use the term.

1854 James and Charlotte Sweet House
[University of the Incarnate Word Campus]

The Sweet Homestead was built by Kampmann for James and Charlotte Sweet for fifty-two hundred dollars on land located near the headwaters of the San Antonio River. The simple one-story stone house with basement was the first permanent house built in what would become the city of Alamo Heights and was a good expression of Kampmann's regional vernacular style.

The site was always a controversial one. In December 1837, the city council had passed an ordinance providing for the sale of public lands at auction, the proceeds to be used for public improvements. Sweet, who moved from Canada to San Antonio in 1849, was a partner in a successful mercantile business and was elected alderman in 1852. That same year the City approved the sale of Lots 30 and 31 on the François Giraud survey map of land granted to San Antonio by the Spanish Crown. These lots were sold to Alderman James R. Sweet, against the advice of City Engineer Giraud, who felt that such important real estate should not fall into private ownership. For a price tag of $1,475, Sweet acquired twenty-four acres, located 2.5 miles north of the city. After some legal maneuvering, Sweet added Lot 32 to his acreage, thus acquiring the springs that were the headwaters of the San Antonio River. Sweet now owned the

Fig 10. James and Charlotte Sweet House, 1854. Kampmann typically raised the living space over the basement, making the house cooler, lighter, and providing storage space. This also enhanced the visual image by releasing it from the ground so it appeared to float on a plinth like a Greek temple. [Craig Blount]

source of San Antonio's water supply and its greatest natural resource. Besides losing a crucial public resource to private hands, the fact that those private hands belonged to an elected official raised great debate. He also got a great deal, financing the purchase with the city until 1902.[7]

Sweet survived the scandal; he was elected mayor of San Antonio five times between 1855 and 1863. As mayor, he sold himself an additional sixty acres. Sweet immediately began planning to build on his initial purchase, contracting with Kampmann in April, 1854, to build "at the head of the San Antonio River a dwelling house" he referred to as the "Sweet Homestead" or the "Old Sweet Place" to be completed by November of that year.[8]

The Sweet House was a hall and parlor house raised a few feet above a basement level, similar to the Dashiell House, as well as to Kampmann's own house begun the same year. This house had a more formal but still vernacular Greek Revival appearance. The hipped roof extended to shelter a full-width front porch with a ratio of 1:5:1. Six piers supported the porch, creating five spatial squares across the façade. These squares framed two sets of tall double-hung sash windows and a central entry. The rectangular front door was framed on either side by four-paned side-lights atop wooden piers and five square transom lights, an ensemble forming another visual square. The plan is laid out around a full-length central hallway with a chimneyed hall and parlor on either side. On both sides of the house were octagonal rooms, creating a well-lit and elegant dining room and parlor.

A central approach to the symmetrical house led to a front porch raised over the basement level. The paneled front door was surrounded by side-lights that were connected across the top of the doorway by a row of five square panes. The entrance was flanked by tall double-hung sash windows almost as tall as the door, all bringing light into the interior and aligned with interior passages and windows at the rear, giving the house ventilation. The thick walls also insulated the house against both heat and cold. A five-bay front porch ran the full width of the façade and was deep enough for rocking chairs on a warm evening. The shaded porch, raised basement, and shallow hipped roof emphasized the horizontality of the house and kept it low to the ground. All of these features combined to give the house a very formal presence, typical of the one-story antebellum Greek Revival build-ings popular in the United States, but much more informal than the two-story Greek Revival plantation houses found throughout the South.

The Sweets sold this property (including water rights) to Gerald Barnes for $3,000 in 1859 and eventually consolidated their holdings into a large parcel of prime land that became the seeds of the city of Alamo Heights. George W. Brackenridge purchased the entire Sweet property from Barnes a decade later for $4,500 under his mother Isabella's name. He lived with his mother and sister in the Sweet House while they built the adjacent three-story English mansion, completed between 1886 and 1889.

Fig 11 (left). The well-lit basement was accessible from the front of the house, under the porch. [author]

Fig 12 (below). View from the rear shows how placement and size of windows brought in light, circulated air, and made the rooms more elegant. [author]

Fig 13. The Sweet House currently serves as office space at the University of the Incarnate Word. [author]

Brackenridge, who also owned the San Antonio National Bank, financed much of the private Water Works Company being developed by Jean Baptiste Lacoste. He bought shares in the company, extended credit to it, and by 1879, was its majority stockholder and president.[9] Following the death of his mother in 1897, Brackenridge sold the 108-acre parcel for $100,00 to the Sisters of the Charity of the Incarnate Word, with the provision that the buildings and grounds be maintained.[10] The University now uses the Sweet House as office space.

1854 François des Mazieres House
601 S. Alamo [322 Martinez]

François Louis des Mazieres built a store building at Martinez and South Alamo Streets in 1853, and the following year added the two-story house next door to the west on Martinez Street, separated by a gated driveway.

Fig 14. The des Mazieres store (left) and house (right) [Marvin Eickenroht, 1934, Library of Congress, Prints and Photographs Division, Historic American Buildings Survey HABS TEX, 15-SANT, 2-1]

The second story of the store was used as a gaming room, which is probably what spurred the family to build the house next door.[11]

Kampmann was the stonemason for the residence. The house was built of limestone laid in random courses varying from 8–12 feet high and plastered inside and out. The exterior walls were plastered with lime plaster and whitewashed to set off the Texas cypress woodwork. The front façade had a four-bay covered walkway created by the gallery across the second floor. Two center doors bifurcated the front façade and separated two windows that cross-ventilated the house. All doors and windows featured similar shutters. The pattern of two doors and two windows was repeated at the back, but with a different arrangement (see fig. 15). A gabled roof covered with split cypress shingles capped the house.[12]

The height of the two-story house was aligned with his store, separated by a small gated space. The ornamental gallery read as an extension of the plain galleries on the hipped-roof storefront (fig. 14).[13] This gave the two buildings a Monterey Colonial appearance, which was, in fact, how it was

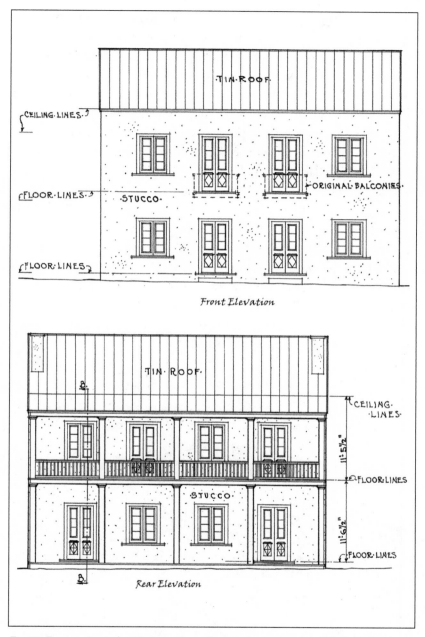

Fig 15. Francois Louis des Mazieres House, front and rear elevations [M.C. Frederick, 1934, HABS TEX, 15-SANT, 2-2]

described by Marvin Eichenreht, HABS (Historic American Buildings Survey) San Antonio District Officer for the project, in 1934.[14]

The first floor consisted of four rooms that opened onto one another with two doors opening onto the front porch (fig. 17). Both front rooms had fireplaces, and the symmetrical arrangement of the space allowed rooms to be closed off so both sides could be rented, which is what happened to the building later. Upstairs were two large bedrooms that ran the full thirty-foot depth of the house. A single door separated them, but both rooms had doors and windows opening onto the gallery that aligned with windows at the back to allow for cross ventilation. These two large rooms were later divided into four rooms and a hall. There were no windows along either side of the house.

Interior walls were plastered and painted with cypress trim. The handmade solid wood panel doors were connected by mortise and tenon with wood dowels. All newel posts, sashes, moldings, and trim in the house were hand-carved solid cypress.[15] It was rumored that this house contained the first bathtub in the city, frequently causing strangers to knock on the front door to examine this curiosity.[16]

Fig 16. The des Mazieres House [Marvin Eickenroht, 1934, HABS TEX, 15-SANT, 2-3]

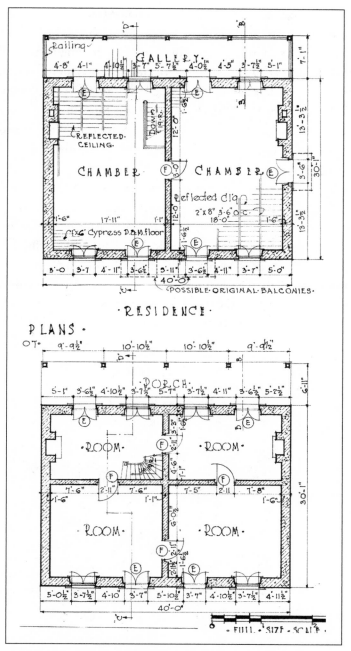

Fig 17. The des Mazieres House plan [Addis E. Noonan, 1934, HABS TEX, 15-SANT, 2-1]

Des Mezieres died in 1862, leaving the buildings to his siblings. Prior to Texas's secession, the buildings were occupied by General David E. Twiggs, with the store next door serving as his office.[17] According to Sarah Eagar, who lived nearby, General Twiggs entertained lavishly, and it was here that Robert E. Lee made the famous remark, "If Virginia secedes, I go with her."[18] On February 16, 1861, Twiggs emerged from the front door and voluntarily and peacefully surrendered Fort Sam Houston to Confederate troops, which was purportedly followed by riots in the streets.[19]

In 1905, Captain J. E. Elgin acquired the property, and by 1934 he was using the downstairs of the store as a saloon.[20] Additions included a two-story wooden bathroom on the rear southern façade. The canti-levered porch, or gallery, on the store was originally supported by iron braces; the first-story posts were put in by Elgin. He also filled in the original space between the two buildings in 1922, changing the external proportions seen in subsequent photographs.[21] The store building was demolished by 1976, but the residence remains standing, though altered; part of the original gallery is missing. It now serves as an office building.

Fig 18. The des Mazieres House is now occupied by law offices [author]

1856 J. Y. Dashiell House
511 Villita Street [Fig Tree Restaurant]

Col. J. Y. Dashiell (1804–1888) earned a medical degree from the University of Maryland at the age of nineteen. He then practiced medicine in Louisville, Kentucky, where he was one of the founders of the Louisville Medical College, and in Princeton, Mississippi. He enlisted in the US Army in July 1846, and served as army paymaster and as a member of General William Jenkins Worth's staff during the Mexican War, stationed in San Antonio.

In 1849, he purchased a lot with a house on it on Villita between the street and the river for $600 from (future mayor) Parquin L. Buquor, with whom the Dashiell family stayed while the new house was built.[22] According to daughter Aurelia Dashiell, she was to oversee the building of a house, redoing the frame house built by Buquor, on a budget of $3,000. Dashiell wrote to his daughter that he felt this sum was reasonable, as prices in San Antonio were higher by one-third than in Charleston or even New York. The contract with Kampmann specified that two-thirds of that fee would be made in seven equal installments over the next eight months, with the final third due "when the work is done to satisfaction." James Vance was to approve any plans as he "valued his judgement [sic] highly in matters of labor and materials." Dashiell requested water be piped into the house, wisely specifying that "pipes be in place before the plastering was done." He suggested that the existing frame house be converted into a kitchen and servants' quarters, and the new construction be "a soft rock house, 33 x 33 x 30 feet high [. . .] giv[ing] Mrs. Dashiell eight rooms."[23]

What the Dashiells got from Kampmann was a rectangular limestone house covered with stucco and capped with a hipped roof. The single-story house was built atop a raised basement. The plain vernacular front was built for function, not style. A wide porch extended across the front of the house with four tall doors leading into the house. The basement opened to a garden in the rear, which extended down to the river just where it turned, creating a pastoral view. The house had cross-ventilation providing a pleasant breeze, and it was kept cool in the summer and warm in the winter by thick limestone walls. It was considered one of the most beautiful houses in the La Villita neighborhood.[24] The

Fig 19 Col. Jeremiah Dashiell House, ca. 1922-24, before restoration [101-61 University of Texas at San Antonio Special Collections (UTSA SC)]

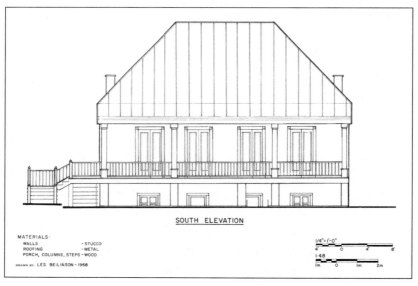

SOUTH ELEVATION

MATERIALS·
WALLS   - STUCCO
ROOFING   - METAL
PORCH, COLUMNS, STEPS - WOOD

DRAWN BY: LES BEILINSON - 1968

1/4"=1'-0"

1:48

Fig 20. Dashiell House elevation [Les Beilinson, 1968, HABS TEX, 15-SANT, 37]

Dashiells' slave, Mary, cooked and lived in the old frame house, which had been converted into a kitchen and servant's quarters, separated from the main house.[25]

Dashiell didn't live in the house very long. He was dismissed from the

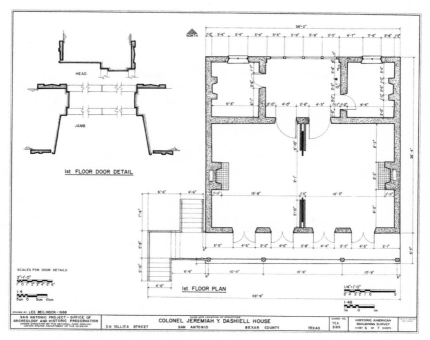

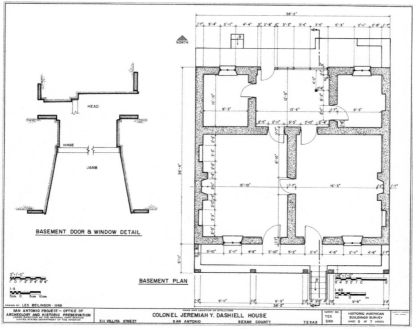

Fig 21 (top). Dashiell House plan first floor [Les Beilinson, 1968, HABS TEX, 15-SANT, 37]Fig 22 (bottom). Dashiell House plan basement [Les Beilinson, 1968, HABS TEX, 15-SANT, 37]

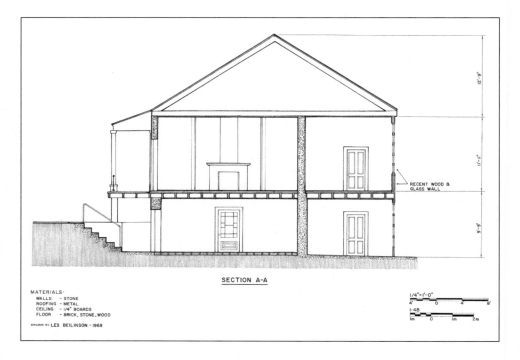

Fig 23 (above). Dashiell House section [Les Beilinson, 1968, HABS TEX, 15-SANT, 37] Fig 24 (below). Dashiell House restored [Les Beilinson, 1969, HABS TEX, 15-SANT, 37-1]

US Army on July 10, 1858, when a boat carrying $23,000 in gold sank under his command. He stayed in San Antonio as part owner of the San Antonio *Herald* newspaper.[26] Unfortunately he lost the house in 1860, forced to sell it due to bankruptcy caused by the $10,818.22 debt he still owed the US government. The house was sold at auction for thirty-four hundred dollars.[27] Dashiell later served in the Confederate army as adjutant general and quartermaster general from November 11, 1861, to January 1862, and as adjutant general and inspector general from 1862 to the end of the war.

The property went through a number of hands and was rented out to both residential and commercial tenants in the twentieth century. The 1921 flood damaged the ground floor considerably.[28] In 1942, the San Antonio Conservation Society (SACS) acquired the building for $7,000. Although the detached kitchen and stable were gone by then, they restored the house and garden.

Renovation required painting, plastering, new floors and plumbing, and a new bathroom, all overseen by O'Neil Ford.[29] From 1953 to 1974, "Casa Villita" served as SACS headquarters in La Villita. The national preservation lobby "Preservation Action" was founded here in 1974, and planner Sam Zisman, who frequently collaborated with O'Neil Ford, had his office in the basement. The building was later leased to the Fig Tree Restaurant. The landmark building was included in the "La Villita Historic District" nomination to the National Register of Historic Places in 1972, and featured on the 1983 NIOSA poster.[30]

1860 Gustav Blersch House
213 Washington St.

Kampmann repeated the vernacular German-Texas pattern in the 1860 Gustav Blersch House at 213 Washington in King William, with a backyard leading to the river. Kampmann built the house, which was designed by Gustave Friesleben. The house was built of wood instead of limestone block and featured a modified Greek Revival front porch spanning the

Fig 25. Gustav Blersch House, ca. 1860 [Library of Congress LC-US262-954405]

Fig 26. Blersch House [author]

façade. The center bay was capped by a low-pitched gable and segmental arch, revealing a modified Federal doorway with sidelights and three square/rectangular panels across the top (see figs. 25–26). The masonry walls were stuccoed, and instead of a gabled roof, this house had a flat roof. A parapet with an entablature formed the cornice behind the porch and framed the verandah, which had wooden piers with simple capitals and a lattice pattern, but the trim was more delicate than in Kampmann's previous houses. The overall effect gave the house a softened Greek Revival appearance.

The L-shaped plan was much like Kampmann's own house. The

main living space was raised up a few feet over a half-buried basement, making it appear to be floating. The extension on the right hand side allowed additional light into the house, which was occupied by the Blersch family until 1871.

1860s John and Regina Beckmann House #3
116 Casino St [demolished]

John Conrad Beckmann (1815–1907) and his wife, Regina (1815–1905), were early immigrants to San Antonio, perhaps as early as 1840. According to family history, the Catholic Beckmann was forbidden to marry his Swiss Protestant fiancée, so the two eloped to New York in 1841.[31] He had trained in Zurich as a locksmith and ironworker doing "fancy/artistic ironwork."[32]

After experimenting with farming in Helotes and battling Indians, he joined his wife, who had stayed in San Antonio, where he opened the first blacksmith shop in the city on the southwest corner of Commerce and Casino. He worked as a blacksmith at the Alamo during the US Army's renovations of the building, and also fabricated iron bedsteads—a skill taught to him by Dr. Ferdinand Herff. Beckmann was a Mason (as was Kampmann) and active in many German-American associations, including the German-English School and the Casino Club (see chapter 4) where the Beckmanns celebrated their fiftieth anniversary in 1891.

In the late 1850s, the Beckmanns built their third house, located at 116 Casino near his shop, on a large lot that sloped down to the river, purchased from Jacob Waelder. Kampmann was commissioned to build what Vinton Lee James described as "a pretty rock residence" and "very large and almost palatial."[33] Steinfeldt described it as being of "sturdy quality [. . .] suggest[ing] comfort and endurance" (see fig. 27).[34] The boxy one-story L-shaped house was set back about thirty-five feet on Casino Street across the street from the Casino Club (see fig. 35). It was

Fig 27. John Conrad and Regina Beckmann House [Thomas W. Cutrer, 81-506 UTSA SC]

approximately forty-four by thirty-five feet, with a half-basement below the main structure, making it very similar in appearance to Kampmann's house, except the porch was centered and not extended, and the house was narrower.[35]

The front yard featured a flower stand that began its life as a wrought candle chandelier designed by Beckmann for the Casino Club. The Beckmann family lived in this house until 1902, shortly before their deaths.[36] By 1910, the building served as Mrs. Alice Howard's Rooming House; it was razed in 1926.[37] The foundation may still be there, but the lots were altered by construction and filled during the 1939 river beautification project. In the mid-1940s, the site became the home of Casa Rio, the first restaurant on the river and pioneer of the dining barges.[38]

1868 Ball Houses
18-22 [116, 120] King William Street

Stoneworkers and brothers Joseph and John Ball moved to San Antonio from the small community of Elmendorf. John went to work for Kampmann as a stonemason, and in about 1868, working with Kampmann, the brothers built nearly identical homes next door to each other on King William Street. Joseph lived at 18 [now 116] and John at 22 [120]. The matching houses, set back from the street ten feet, were small German vernacular cottages amid the Victorian oleo of sizes and styles along that street, which was rapidly becoming the center of the nineteenth-century German community. Joseph's house has been substantially altered, including the addition of a second story and gingerbread detailing in 1903, but John's house retains its original character (see fig. 28). The side-gable

Fig 28. John and Catherine Ball House [author]

was elongated to cover an eight-foot-wide front porch, originally built of wood, which extended across the thirty-six-foot façade of the nearly square building and added considerably to the living space. A lean-to in the back kept the roofline symmetrical. In the local German farm or ranch tradition, there were two front doors in the center of the porch and two vertical windows on either side of the set of doors. One door led to the hall and the other to the parlor. Behind these rooms were a kitchen and bedroom. The house sat on a stone foundation with load-bearing stone walls twelve to sixteen inches thick, both sides plastered over, which kept the house cool, as did the tall attic space and the eleven and a half feet height of the rooms. Ceilings were originally suspended canvas, and there was a stone-walled cellar below the southeast corner of the house.

The floor line was raised up to about fifteen inches above grade. Not only did this protect the house from the threat of flooding, but it also helped with ventilation and gave the house the illusion of a plinth. Located in the northern wall at the front left was a chimney. Legend has it that this wall facing his brother's house originally had no windows, due to a feud between the two wives. While Joseph and his wife, Sallie, moved away, John and Catherine stayed for many years, and windows were eventually added.

1869 Charles Philip and Elizabeth Degen House
348 E. Crockett [demolished]

German immigrant Charles Phillip Degen began his professional career in San Antonio as brewmaster for William and Mary Menger's Western Brewery, a small establishment located in the basement of the Menger Hotel (built by Kampmann in 1859; see chapter 4) on Alamo Plaza. Established in 1855, this was the first brewery in San Antonio.[39] Beer was kept cold by the acéquia flowing through the building—the Acéquia Madre or "Mother Ditch." Degen continued operating the brewery after Menger's death in 1871 until it closed in 1878. By then it was the largest operating brewery in Texas.[40]

Besides establishing the standard for beer production in San Antonio, Degen was a strong presence in the community, especially in the German community. He was a founder and served as treasurer of the San Antonio Beneficiary Association [*Kronkenkassen Verein*], an organization providing medical and funeral benefits to its members from 1858 through at least 1895.[41] He was the oldest volunteer fire fighter in San Antonio and a member of Bexar Encampment No. 11, the Order of Odd Fellows, Alamo Lodge #206, and Knights and Ladies of Honor. He was often listed as honorary pallbearer in obituaries.[42]

In 1860, Degen (age thirty-five) married Elizabeth Fink (age twenty-one), a social butterfly, well known locally for her accomplishments in horticulture, and eventual leader of several charity organizations, including president of the German Ladies Society for thirty-five years.[43] In 1868, the Degens bought two lots on Crockett Street. Kampmann was commissioned to build a one-story stone house at 348 Crockett, completed the following year. The Degens lived here for thirty-four years, raising eight children in this house.[44]

The house was a small, square limestone building, with a five-bay porch trimmed with Victorian gingerbread and a flat roof. A small bathroom was added in the rear sometime before 1904. A small reception room opened into the dining room, which Degen considered the most important place in the house, as it was filled with antiques that he had acquired.[45]

In 1878, when Western Brewery ceased operations, the Degens added a rock brewery behind their house, at 237 Blum Street, adjacent to and sharing a garden with the house. They purchased Menger's equipment and began producing "Degen's Beer." The beverage was to be consumed on site, never shipped, not even to nearby hotels and restaurants. Despite this limitation, it was still a very lucrative business. Tables and chairs were set up in one room and the other room housed the vats where the dark brown beer was brewed. Degen was not interested in enlarging the business, but rather was satisfied with a small hometown business, never producing more than two barrels a day. Contemporary newspapers described "Goin' to Degen's" as a common cultural pastime, especially for celebratory occasions. Visitors came to the "one-man brewery" from as far as Vermont to sip the heavy beer from large mugs, which sold for five cents, and to watch it being made in the next room. He refused numerous offers to expand or purchase the brewery or to acquire the recipe. "It is not what you put in the beer," he said, "but how you brew it that makes it what it is."[46] In 1908, the Federal Agriculture Department reported, "Degen's brew was purer than any other in the United States."[47] Contemporary literature described it as "the healthiest beer in the country" and claimed the US Health Department proclaimed it as a "cure for tuberculosis."[48]

Charles Degen died in 1912, at age the age of eighty-seven, but the house stayed in the family until 1921. Front and rear porches were added in 1892. His son Louis continued to operate the brewery, selling bottled beer by the case until impending Prohibition forced the closure of the business. When the family sold the house on Crockett Street to a taxi company in order to settle the estate, the old brewery building behind it became a storage space for their furniture. The house was demolished in 1953 to create a parking lot for Joske's, later replaced by the Rivercenter Mall. When a parking garage was added to the mall in 1999, an archaeological investigation of the site revealed that the house was, indeed, well built:

> The foundations of the house were substantially constructed, two feet wide, of shaped limestone with larger stones at corners and occasionally along the wall lines. A two-inch footing of limestone rubble was laid in the wall trench, upon which the foundations were laid up with soft sand as mortar. The stones that formed the chimney base were larger than those in the rest of the foundations, and projected about 12" from the inner wall line.[49]

1870 Sarah and Robert Eagar House
434 S. Alamo

Sarah Elizabeth Riddle, daughter of one of the first Anglo families to settle permanently in San Antonio, was born in 1841, on the site where the Aztec Theatre now stands. In 1866, she married Robert Eagar, who had come to San Antonio from Halifax, Nova Scotia, thinking he would hunt buffalo based on an ad in a New York paper, but, instead, worked as a bookkeeper at Vance Brothers. He later became a trader and broker. Shortly after their marriage, Robert and Sarah commissioned Kampmann to build their house at 434 S. Alamo on land that had been in her family for many years and was originally part of the Alamo farmland.[50] They agreed to a sum of $4,821 in December 1869, although the debt was extended several times and not released until 1894. They raised three daughters there. Eagar was a Mason in Lodge #44, which is probably where he met fellow Mason John Kampmann. By this time, Kampmann was calling himself an architect and builder and was listed as such in the San Antonio Business Index (see stationery in fig. 29–30).

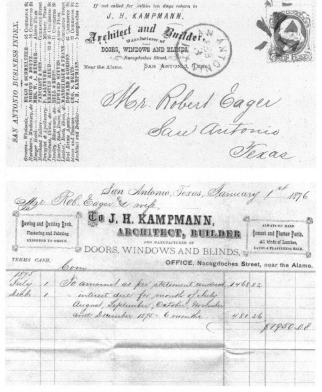

Fig 29 (top). Kampmann's stationery [courtesy of David Carter]
Fig 30 (bottom). Statement from Kampmann received by Sarah and Robert Eagar, 1876 [courtesy of David Carter]

The one-story limestone house set back on the lot facing S. Alamo was a classic Texas–German vernacular and Kampmann "rock house."[51] It had a symmetrical five-bay Texas Greek Revival façade with square wooden posts instead of columns, and a stylized entablature at the cornice, topped with a shallow side-facing gabled roof. The porch extended across the width of the house and protected the central entry with a pair of tall shuttered double-hung windows on either side of the paneled door framed in side-lights. The porch was raised four steps in the center and deep enough for sitting and visiting with the neighbors, and created a plinth on which the house sat (see figs. 31–32). At one time there were nine people living in the house—three generations plus a servant and boarder.[52]

At the rear of the house was a small one-story dependency containing two rooms with back-to-back fireplaces in what was called a "saddlebag" or enclosed "dogtrot" plan. It was used as a kitchen and servants' quarters, and later was rented out to boarders.

Fig 31. Sarah and Robert Eagar House, 1866 [author]

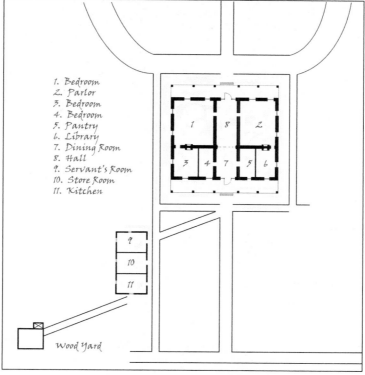

1. Bedroom
2. Parlor
3. Bedroom
4. Bedroom
5. Pantry
6. Library
7. Dining Room
8. Hall
9. Servant's Room
10. Store Room
11. Kitchen

Wood Yard

Fig 32 (top). Eagar House [author] Fig 33 (bottom). Eagar House plan. The house was built to appear symmetrical to the eye, but the inside measurements indicate a slight discrepancy. [Melissa Ramos]

Fig 34. Sarah Eagar lived in the house for almost eight decades, from 1870 until her death in 1947. [courtesy of David Carter]

Sarah was widowed in 1883. For the next sixty-four years, she was always dressed in black, often with a veil, but continued to be very active in the community. She was a founder of the San Antonio de Bexar Chapter of the Daughters of the American Revolution and the Pioneer Club. She served as Custodian of the Alamo for many years (listed in the 1910 Census as her occupation), and was featured in annual celebrations of the Alamo. She was also active in St. Mark's Episcopal Church. She partied with Jefferson Davis and Robert E. Lee and regaled the city residents for years with tales of her adventures—from being kidnapped by Indians in the 1840s to seeing women emancipated in the 1920s.

Sarah Eagar's birthday was an annual social event worthy of note in the newspapers. She held an open house on that day until 1946 when at age 104, she was too weak to entertain. When she died in 1947, at the age of 105 (older than the state of Texas), she left the house to her daughter Florence, who lived there until she died in 1967 at the age of 100. After much negotiation, the San Antonio Conservation Society eventually acquired the home. Unlike many of its neighbors, it was spared demolition for HemisFair in 1968 and used for the Southern Baptist Church Pavilion. After the fair, it was leased as offices, and it has now been restored to serve as the new headquarters for HemisFair Park.

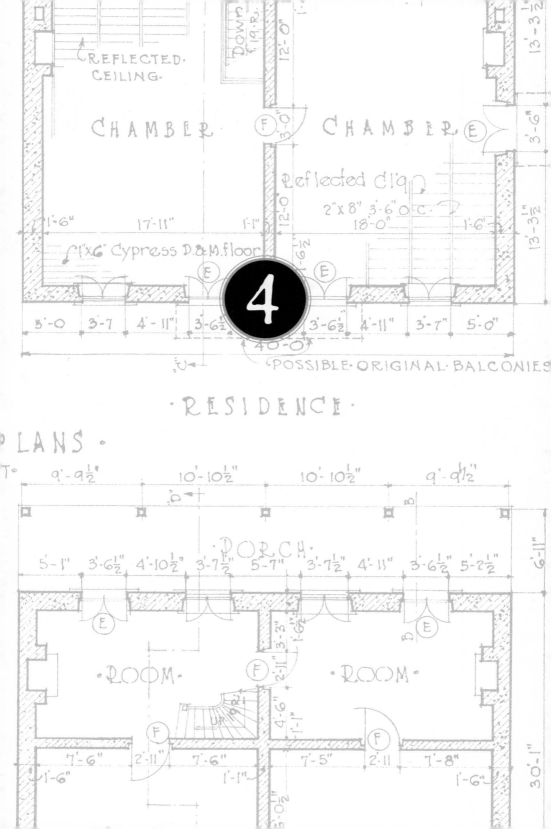

REFLECTED.
CEILING.

DOWN 19 R.

12'-0"

13'-3½"

CHAMBER

F

3'-0"

CHAMBER

E

3'-6"

Reflected cl'g

2"x 8" 3'-6" 0.C.
18'-0"

12'-0"

13'-3½"

1'-6"   17'-11"   1'-1"   1'-6"

-6½

1"x6" Cypress D.& M. floor

E   E

4

5'-0" 3-7 4'-11" 3'-6½"   3'-6½" 4'-11" 3'-7" 5'-0"

40'-0"

POSSIBLE·ORIGINAL·BALCONIES

·RESIDENCE·

PLANS·

9'-9½"   10'-10½"   10'-10½"   9'-9½"

6'-11"

·PORCH·

5'-1" 3'-6½" 4'-10½" 3'-7½" 5'-7" 3'-7½" 4'-11" 3'-6½" 5'-2½"

E

F

3'-3"

-6½

·ROOM·

F

UP 19 R.

4'-6"

·ROOM·

E

F

30'-1"

7'-6" 2'-11" 7'-6"   7'-5" 2-11 7'-8"

1'-6"   1'-1"   1'-6"

German Community Building and Division 1855–1868

))•●•((

Beginning with the *Adelsverein* for new settlers (described in chapter 1), the German-American community in Texas was a tightly knit group that not only survived but thrived by helping each other. This mutual aid attitude started in Germany and continued as they started new towns, such as New Braunfels and Boerne, and settled into existing communities, such as San Antonio. There they built houses and established communities east of the San Antonio River, near the *acéquias*, Alameda [Commerce Street], and Alamo Plaza. They lived in ethnic neighborhoods and joined clubs and groups where they could benefit each other and the larger community. They created new neighborhoods such as King William (originally *Kaiser Wilhelm*—the name was Anglicized during World War I) and added on to older ones like the Irish Flats behind Alamo Plaza.

Always, they maintained traditions that included festivals, food, cultural celebrations, education, and keeping the German language alive for their children. They supported German-language newspapers, sponsored traveling lecturers and performers, and established *vereins* for singing, exercise, and bowling, often competing for trophies with the *vereins* from

---

other German-American communities. They built schools, music halls, and bowling alleys. Johann Kampmann (or John, or occasionally Hermann as he began calling himself) played a major role in these activities in San Antonio both before and after the Civil War. The same names show up repeatedly on membership lists of various organizations, including the name Kampmann. He was an active member, often taking a leadership role, and drew clients from these intertwined communities. His architectural work as developer, client, contractor, materials provider, investor, and designer/architect helped change the public face of San Antonio from its strictly Spanish heritage to one that included Anglo-German, as he had begun doing with private houses.

The *verein* was a strong social tradition in Germany that continued in the United States, especially among newly arrived immigrants. Vereins were voluntary organizations, each focused on promoting a particular cause or encouraging an interest in social, cultural, or religious goals. This included the "Freethinkers," who fought against the endorsement of any official religion and refused to begin a colony by building a church, unlike most European settlers. They established and supported organizations, schools, and charities that contributed to the development of German-American communities in towns and cities throughout the United States in the nineteenth century. They also built many institutions, often open to the public for certain events, in which to house club activities. The facilities were also rented out to other groups to generate income for the club. Turners, as members of the *turnvereins* (gymnastics associations) came to be called, also organized volunteer fire departments and supported other causes to benefit the entire community, not just their own interests.

Kampmann and friends (and past or future clients), including Charles Hummel, Charles Fisher, Judge Jacob Waelder, John Herff, Frederick Herff, Gustav Blersch, Gustave Friesleben, Charles Degen, and John Fries, met at the Hummel Building on November 10, 1852, to discuss organizing an "association for social intercourse" among prominent German businessmen.[1] While it was first named the San Antonio *Schuetzen Verein* (shooting club), by the time the charter was granted in 1857, the name had changed to the Casino-*Gesellschaft*, or Casino Club Association, with 106 charter members—all German and all male.

Membership was originally restricted to "speakers of the mother tongue," but US Army officers in dress uniform were granted guest privileges. It was not to be restricted to the upper class German population, but to be open to anyone "with a sincere interest in the arts."[2] The Casino Club was San Antonio's oldest and certainly its most prominent social club for many years.

The club first met in the Hummel Building on West Commerce until the organization grew too large. Then they met upstairs at a building on the corner of Commerce and Navarro, referred to as the "Kampmann Building," because the Kampmann family lived in the rear portion before their own home on Nacogdoches was ready for occupation. The lower part of the building was member Charles Rossy's mercantile and confectionary store.[3] By the mid-1850s, the club agreed they needed a building of their own, and in 1856 purchased a site on West Market from member Jacob Waelder to build the Casino Hall. Architects and builders Gustave Friesleben, John Fries, and John Kampmann were all on the building committee.

1857 Casino Hall
210 Market Street [demolished]

The architectural design has been attributed to both Casino members Wilhelm Carl August Thielepape (engineer and future mayor) and to John Fries, which is more likely. The construction contract was awarded to Kampmann. The building was financed by the dues-paying members and subscribers, including Edward Steves, who contributed $5,500. It occupied the lot on Market Street that backed up to the river, across the street from John Conrad Beckmann's house (built by John Kampmann that same decade).

The center portion was completed in 1857 and officially inaugurated on January 17, 1858, with an impressive ceremony. The Greek Revival style was typical for buildings requiring a public presence in American cities at that time. The one-story building had a three-bay porch across

Fig 35. Casino Hall is #17; John Beckman's house is across the street on the left-hand side with trees in the front yard. [Augustus Koch Bird's-Eye Map, 1873]

the front and a shallow tympanum rising above, similar to the Menger Hotel's main façade, also built by Fries and Kampmann (see fig. 42). The façade was composed of a central entry flanked by tall windows in the vernacular German tradition. It housed the meeting room/auditorium and a ballroom with a stage and balcony and was ornately decorated in "white and old gold."[4] In 1860, the east wing was added, containing a parlor and lounge for ladies and billiards and a ninepin bowling alley downstairs for men. This was followed in 1864 by the addition of a west wing, which featured more activities for members, including a bar, skat (a popular card game similar to bridge) tables, committee rooms, and a reading room.[5] Members were widely read, as the club subscribed to several international newspapers and had their own personal chairs.

The facilities were open to men on a daily basis, and there were monthly entertainments and celebrations to which the whole family was invited. In the early years, speaking German was a requirement for membership; later that rule was more relaxed, but use of the native tongue was still mandatory for officers. But they also invited the public to lectures and performances and welcomed distinguished visitors to the city, including Generals U.S. Grant and Robert E. Lee, although their visits were a decade apart.

Alamo City author Pearson Newcomb called the Casino Club "the first attractive public building in San Antonio," and Vinton L. James agreed it was "the first beautiful public building" in the city.[6] While that may be an exaggeration, the Greek Revival façade was situated so as to provide a visual terminus on the cross street later named Casino Street, and the back overlooked the river. The front façade had a raised central portion with a front-facing gabled façade with a small squared rise at the peak and flattened corners, all awaiting their Greco-Roman acroteria. Fronting the façade was a tetrastyle porch with wooden columns supporting an architrave. When viewed frontally, the space above the porch formed an illusionary pediment. The three bays of the porch framed by the columns and pilasters behind articulated the entrance and the tall windows on either side. The interior was adorned with four huge gilt-framed mirrors that were from Mrs. Astor's New York mansion. Beckmann contributed a wrought iron candle chandelier that was moved to his own house when the club voted to experiment with gas lighting.[7]

The clubhouse was envisioned as a cultural center. In the free-thinking German tradition, the by-laws, drawn up by Julius Berens and ratified by the original membership, prohibited use of the hall for political or religious purposes. The club sponsored verein activities and hosted rehearsals and practices for the *Männerchor*, Belknap Rifles, and Casino Bowling Team. The club played an important role in establishing a "social season" in the city. Fathers reserved memberships for their sons and formally

Fig 36. Casino Hall in 1892, taken from John Beckmann's front yard [Witteman, 1892]

introduced their daughters at an annual formal event.[8] The season opened in September with a ball and closed in May with a masquerade. In between they celebrated Christmas with a masked ball, Washington's birthday, and Shrove Tuesday (the German version of Mardi Gras). There was also a Fourth of July party and celebrations for Humboldt's birthday, the US Centennial, and, of course, Casino Club anniversaries. "Music was provided by a military band and all ranking officers from the posts always attended in full dress uniform. Supper was served after midnight and champagne was favored."[9]

The biggest event of the year was the New Year's Eve bash. Many a midnight kiss was exchanged between spouses or hopefuls when the lights flickered, signaling the change in the calendar. According to the San Antonio *Light*, the New Year's Eve Masquerade Ball was the most exclusive social function in the city for years. In a schmaltzy paragraph, the paper described the setting:

> From a life-sized picture on the wall, looked out the statesman face of Bismarck, surrounded by diplomats and nobles signing the treaty of peace that closed the hostilities of two nations. [. . .] did the grim face of the old warrior really relax, and his hand extend to grasp a goblet of the golden wine, when each man sprang to his feet, and with joyful shout of "*Hoch stolen sie leben. Hoch stolen sie leben, Drej mal hoch*" drank to the beloved country, and to the men, who though in exile on a new and younger soil, have not forgotten one blade of grass in her Rhine valley, or one purple light on her glorious hills.[10]

In addition to the four hundred-seat auditorium, the space included a full stage, dressing rooms, storage scenery, and permanent sets, so it was always intended to be more than just a lecture hall. Thus, Casino Hall was the first "respectable" theater in the city, even before the Opera House was built on Alamo Plaza thirty years later. Historically, theater options were limited and considered inappropriate for gentlemen and ladies.[11] Most American cities, in fact, had no "legitimate" theaters until the 1820s. Prior to this (and well after), live theater and theater people were considered suspect at best, immoral for sure, and indecent probably. While opera was considered cultural, traveling theater groups conjured up visions of "hoochie-koochie" dancers and bare female flesh, telling tales of no redeeming social value (definitely not suitable for women and children) before the troupes skipped town and ignored the hotel bill. The term "Opera House" was often used to give legitimacy to live entertainment venues.

In San Antonio, live entertainment before the 1850s consisted of religious pageants and *carpas*, in which traveling companies set up circus tents and performed acts and songs in Spanish. In Anglo culture, theater was the polite term for saloon, since most live performances occurred in cheap bars and were a secondary activity to drinking; novel acts detained the drinkers. The German emphasis on family, community, and social aspects of beer drinking in gardens contrasted with whiskey swigging in dark, stinky rooms. There was no place conducive to this in San Antonio when German-Americans arrived.

By 1868, the club had organized their own "little theater" group called the Casino Theater, which included Wilhelm Thielepape, known as the "singing mayor."[12] The stage could also be rented by itinerant troupes for $20 per night plus gas, plus a state license of $7.50 per performance, and $6.50 a week for hotel, including meals.[13] Until 1877, the railroad only went as far as Austin, and performers were known to pay an additional $11 fare to travel to San Antonio by stagecoach in order to perform at the Casino Club.[14] Charles Griesenbeck was the theater manager and issued the warning that all entertainment was to be vetted beforehand. He accepted only shows of "high caliber" and reminded all guests, "The Casino requires an explicit description of the kind of performances to be given before it grants the hall."[15] Proceeds were used to finance club activities and lectures.

The theater was so successful an enterprise that after the arrival of the railroad in 1877, which meant more traveling troupes and more customers, the auditorium was redone, increasing the seating capacity to seven hundred. A new tin roof and ceiling were installed, additional stage scenery and curtains purchased, and the whole building got a new coat of paint.[16]

Casino Hall was considered the "best opera house in San Antonio" with a top price of one dollar admission.[17] During its lifetime it was a highlight of San Antonio culture and a municipal institution. Many booking applications were turned down because the schedule was so crowded.[18] Sidney Lanier included references to the Casino Club in his short stories, and lecturers included Henry Ward Beecher, Carl Schurz, and Buffalo Bill. After the Civil War, the Casino attracted many members from the newly appointed Reconstruction civic government, derided as "Casino Aristocrats" in the press, as though these "outsiders" were vying for legitimacy.

Although beer drinking was a central activity, the Casino bar was not run for profit, and intemperance was not tolerated. Membership, activities, and income all declined sharply after World War I and during Prohibition. Limiting membership to men combined with anti-German sentiment during the war made survival difficult, not to mention that the membership constituted primarily heirs of the original founders. By then, the San Antonio German community no longer needed a club to make them feel included in the larger community, and the club never regained the prominence it enjoyed prewar. The club was in arrears on federal and local taxes. Rentals were down as larger theaters replaced the auditorium, and movies wiped out vaudeville and live performances in the 1920s. In addition to the theatrical competition, the club lost much of its public business during Prohibition.

Members tried to revive it by joining forces with the San Antonio Club, a literary society dating back to 1882, but that did not guarantee survival.[19] The new six-story Art Deco/Mayan Casino Club on West Crockett Street designed by Delwood Co. was built in 1927 to serve the consolidated organizations, but the effort didn't survive the Depression, and the new building went into foreclosure. In 1923, the original Casino building was sold to the San Antonio Water Supply Company to be used as a warehouse, and by 1950, both clubs had been dissolved. The original Casino Club building was abandoned in 1959 and demolished in 1961, when the public library next door, which had been planning to expand and occupy that space, decided instead to move.

1858 Masonic Hall Addition

[1872 Bexar County Courthouse] 114 Soledad

{demolished}

Kampmann joined the Grand Masonic Lodge of Texas following their statewide meeting in San Antonio from January 15–18, 1855, and in August also joined the Masonic Order of the Alamo Lodge No. 44. Freemasonry was a system of morality, separate from any specific religious doctrine, which must have appealed to the German Freethinkers who fled the Revolution of 1848, especially those in the building industries. Freemasonry developed from the eighteenth-century craft guild system and celebrated rational idealism based on freedom of thought and action, based on moral principles of public and private conduct. The Alamo Lodge No. 44 had been established with eight charter members in 1847; by 1858, there were 104 members meeting on the first Saturday of each

Fig 37. Masonic Hall with addition, ca. 1870s [Thomas W. Cutrer 81-502 UTSA SC]

month at the Masonic Hall, located at 114 Soledad. J.H. Kampmann and John M. Campbell were awarded the contract for building an addition to the overcrowded three-story lodge building. The San Antonio *Herald* noted, "From the well-known energy of these gentlemen we have no doubt the work will be pushed rapidly forward."[20]

By 1872, the Masons were in debt, and the Bexar County Courthouse was in need of space. The old "Bat Cave" on Military Plaza, built by Fries and Kampmann two decades before, was too small and in very bad shape, so the county purchased the Masonic Hall on October 3, 1872, for $1,500 in gold and currency. However, the amount was still insufficient to pay off the Masons' debt. Kampmann was again contracted for the addition of a two-story structure to support the county clerk on the lower level and the district clerk on the upper floor. The fireproof addition cost $13,980 for excavation, masonry, and ironwork.[21]

1859 German-English School
421 S. Alamo

One of the primary goals of the Casino Club was the establishment of a school, which would include German culture but not push religious education. Some of the same German businessmen who organized the Casino Club and the Masonic Hall met at the "old Klepper [sic] Hotel to discuss the inadequacy of educational opportunities for the children."[22] They agreed a *Lateiner* school (a scholastic organization based on the study of Latin) was necessary in San Antonio so German-American children could also benefit from the preservation of German language and culture, and receive a proper (rigorous) German education. As with the Casino Club Association, the founders were careful to restrict religious activity. In fact, the club was an official sponsor of the school, and club member Julius Berens was its first director. There were only two public schools at the time, one for boys and one for girls; the other schools were Catholic.

Rule number one established at their first meeting in 1855 prohibited any religious instruction, and rule number two required that the German and English languages be on an equal footing, with lessons taught in both tongues. Rule number three declared, "These principles are hereby emphatically declared organic ones," adding that if either were violated or changed, association members could claim repayment of their subscriptions.[23] The original founders pledged $3,040 for the school and bought two lots on South Alamo from Adele and François Giraud. Pledges were made in the form of quotas, which ranged from thirty to one hundred dollars with 10% down, and the balance due in twelve months.[24] Soon, there were fifty subscribers, most of whom were also on the roster of the Casino Club, who by themselves donated a total of $3,720 to get the school started.[25]

Fig 38. German-English School brochure [courtesy of David Carter]

The first classes were held in rented rooms of the Klöpper Hotel above Nic Tengg's Bookstore on West Commerce (whose store was a successor to Julius Berens's Newspapers & Fancy Goods). The first year, there were two teachers (one English and one German) and fourteen students divided into two classes by age.[26] The names of the students read like a "who's who" of the German community and included the families of many former and future Kampmann clients.[27] The school always admitted girls and hired both male and female (married and single) teachers.

John Kampmann, one of the original subscribers and trustees, was awarded the building contract for the new facility, designed by City Engineer and Surveyor Gustave Friesleben. The cornerstone was laid November 10, 1859, in a ceremony that dedicated the building to poet Friedrich von Schiller on his centennial anniversary. The German-English School was officially incorporated in 1860, with a twenty-year charter from the state. The original members of the Board of Trustees were C. N. Riotte, lawyer and diplomat; Dr. August Nette, pharmacist; W. Friedrich; Gustav Theissen, merchant and alderman; J. H. Kampmann; Gustave Friesleben, city engineer and surveyor; Julius Berens, teacher and bookstore owner; and W.C.A. Thielepape, artist and twice mayor of San Antonio. All were born and educated in Germany, were accomplished scholars in their fields, and set a high standard for the school. [28]

The first structure was three rooms long on the north side of the lot; three more rooms were added in a second building, creating a central courtyard between them. Those buildings were expanded by the addition of a wing and a second floor. The third and final building was added in 1869, completing the horseshoe-shaped campus. The dedication was celebrated at the Casino Club with a grand ball, to which the entire community was invited.[29]

The three stone-and-brick structures were each one room deep and one to two stories tall, capped by gabled roofs. The two parallel buildings had second-floor galleries extending the length of the façades and accessed by external wooden staircases. Classrooms emptied onto the galleries in the German vernacular building tradition; there were no interior corridors. These were vernacular "rock buildings" constructed of locally quarried limestone and mortar, laid in a random pattern.

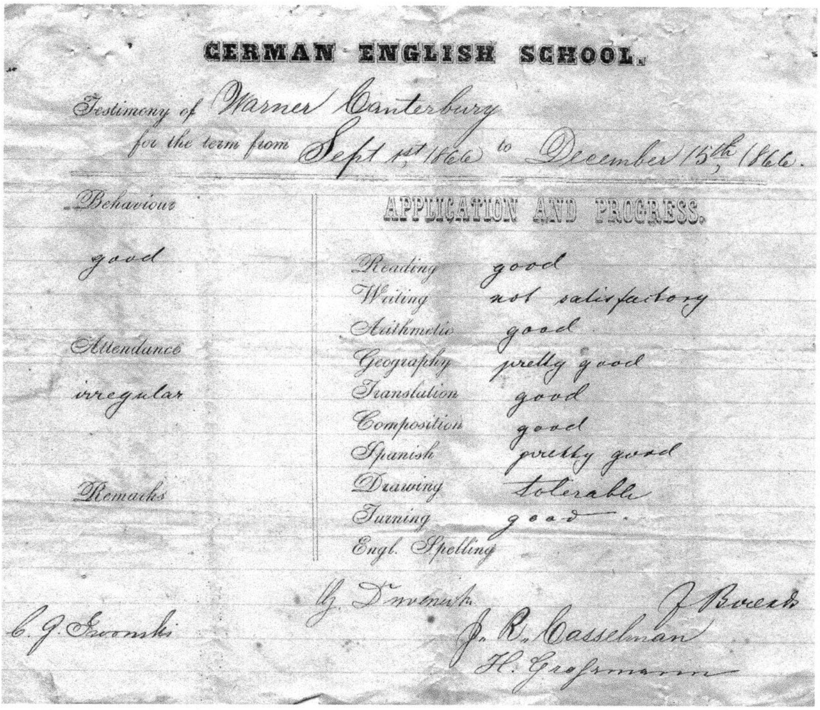

GERMAN ENGLISH SCHOOL.

Testimony of Warner Canterbury
for the term from Sept 1st 1866 to December 15th 1866.

Behaviour
good

Attendance
irregular

Remarks

APPLICATION AND PROGRESS.

Reading good
Writing not satisfactory
Arithmetic good
Geography pretty good
Translation good
Composition good
Spanish pretty good
Drawing tolerable
Turning good.
Engl. Spelling

C. G. Iwonski
J. R. Casselman
H. Grossmann

Fig 39. Report card, dated 1866 [courtesy of David Carter]

Lessons were rigorous. Classes met for six days a week from eight a.m. to five p.m., and the term lasted eleven months. (August was just too hot!) Students followed a strict curriculum with public examinations, and rules were enforced by the use of "frequent and heavy beatings administered with a leather-covered rod."[30] Classes included English, German, Spanish, algebra, geography, writing, history, astronomy, poetry, and gymnastics. Art and swimming were optional, and sewing and cooking were included for female students. Adult classes were held in the evening.[31] Tuition was $2.50 per semester for lower-level classes, and $4.50 for advanced classes, but poor students were allowed to attend for free. Strict rules of deportment written by the board governed student behavior and instilled respect for education.

In the 1860s, enrollment reached its peak, the bills were paid, and the board voted to purchase the adjoining property and expand. Students were being turned away due to lack of space, while city schools were

Fig 40. German-English School [author]

closing due to a lack of funding for teacher salaries.[32] German-English School graduates were being accepted to prestigious eastern schools.

However, as the decade progressed, families moved away, the enrollment as well as the tuition dropped, and public schools were established in each ward. By the 1870s, the school was in financial decline, despite frequent fundraisers sponsored by the Casino Club.[33] In 1886, the school negotiated a low-interest loan, but by 1890, it fell victim to decreased contributions and an improved public education in San Antonio. The property was mortgaged that year to A. B. Frank, Henry Elmendorf, and Albert Maverick. In 1897, the board was forced to sell the property to Frederick Groos & Co., bankers; Hulda Groos; and George W. Brackenridge for $4,505. The buyers paid off the debt. In 1903, the Grooses sold their shares to Brackenridge who, in turn, sold the property to the San Antonio Independent School District. The city maintained it as a school for many years: as Brackenridge Grammar School until 1923, as Thomas Nelson Page Junior High

School from 1923–25, and as the original campus of San Antonio Junior College from 1926–1951. From 1964 to 1968, after restoration, it was the headquarters for HemisFair and was the first building to be restored in La Villita. Championed by O'Neil Ford, it set a precedent for trying to salvage older buildings for the Fair (including Kampmann's Eagar and Halff Houses). When Alamo Street was widened in 1967 in preparation for the Fair, Beethoven Hall and the front yards on the east side of the street were shaved, while the street curved to protect the German-English School on the west side of Alamo at Ford's suggestion.

Since HemisFair, the building has served as a meeting space for various groups and events. In 1992, it was the site of the signing of the North American Fair Trade Agreement Treaty (NAFTA), attended by Prime Minister Brian Mulroney of Canada and Presidents George H. W. Bush of the United States and Carlos Salinas of Mexico.

Fig 41. The school served as headquarters for HemisFair in 1968, and was the backdrop for the signing of the North American Fair Trade Agreement (NAFTA) in 1992. [author]

1859 Menger Hotel
204 Alamo Plaza

Mary Baumschlueter arrived in San Antonio by ox cart from Galveston in 1846 with her mother, who died shortly thereafter. Mary married Emil Guenther, a butcher, but was widowed within a year and running a small boarding house on Commerce Street. One of her boarders was a recent German immigrant, William Menger, a cooper who was operating a brewery on Alamo Plaza. They joined forces, marrying in 1851 and merging their enterprises as well. They built a larger boarding house at Blum and Bonham Streets, with a dining room open to the public, and established the Western Brewery next door in 1855, the first commercial brewery in San Antonio and possibly in Texas. They hired Charles Phillip Degen the following year to serve as brewmaster so they could focus on operation of the business, which included a dining room and a beer garden.

Beer was the German beverage of choice, and beer gardens served as meeting places for social gatherings as well as the site of the beginnings of many businesses and civic organizations. Both the brewery and the boarding house were successful, and in 1858, the Mengers expanded the boarding house into a hotel one hundred yards south of the Alamo facing the Plaza with a new brewery adjacent (see fig. 42). They hired John Fries to design the new structure and his former partner John Kampmann to oversee construction.

Western Brewery was the literal and figurative foundation of the Menger Hotel. According to HABS documentation, the hotel was built of materials salvaged from the wrecking of the old Menger Brewery.[34] German beer was served very cold, unlike English beer. The Mengers stored their beer in a vaulted storage area in the basement, insulated with three-foot-thick stone walls. It was kept chilled by the Alamo Madre Ditch, which ran through the site of the new hotel (what is now the patio).

The Greek Revival hotel was completed February 1, 1859, at a cost of between $15,000 and $16,000.[35] Cut limestone from a local quarry (later the site of Sunken Gardens) was used to construct the two-story,

Fig 42. The Menger Hotel soon after it opened in 1859. [Library of Congress]

fifty-room inn.[36] Ventilated stables housed the guests' horses. The Menger was the first elegant hotel in San Antonio, described in the San Antonio *Herald* shortly before completion:

> The main room on the second floor is unsurpassed for beauty. [. . .] The walls and ceilings unite the smoothness of glass to the whiteness of alabaster, whilst the moldings are conceived in fine taste and executed in the best style of art.[37]

On opening day, January 31, 1859 (only twenty-three years after the Battle of the Alamo), the *Herald* lauded the building's "commanding appearance [. . .] comfortable rooms and plenty of fresh air."[38] The paper also lauded the fact that the first-class hotel would attract businesses to move from Main and Military Plazas to the new downtown.

The hotel faced Alamo Plaza, giving it a nice setback from the street and an open space for guests. Carriages could arrive and depart from in front of the hotel without disturbing traffic. There was also a landscaped area behind the hotel where people could gather. The façade had a three-bay organization with an entablature across the whole of the cornice and a small pediment above the projected central section, similar to that of the Casino Club (see fig. 36). Guests' horses and carriages were kept in a stable on Blum Street, east of the hotel, between St. Joseph's and Bonham Street.

The hotel was an immediate success, and the Mengers added a three-story addition behind the main building next to the garden that summer with forty more rooms between the hotel and the brewery, nearly doubling the capacity. Kampmann was once again the construction manager, and the project was completed September 13, 1859, at a cost of over twenty thousand dollars. The Menger was soon attracting the most notable visitors to the city, who now had a place to stay overnight in luxury. It also drew plenty of locals in the late afternoons, partly because of the food and patio garden, and partly because of the beer. The Menger was credited with encouraging rapid growth of the city in the next decade, as travelers preferred these pleasant accommodations to stopping elsewhere, where they were uncertain what they would find.[39] Special guests were invited on tours of the brewery through a tunnel that opened off the basement. In fact, it was suggested in 1940 that the tunnel and catacombs would make a good bomb shelter if San Antonio were to be attacked. "The Menger hotel would be a very fine place for it has a bar as well as very deep and ancient vaults, formerly used to store beer and liquors."[40] Interiors were lush and all the rooms had high ceilings. The restaurant, named the Colonial Dining Room, was known for its cuisine, including game, mango ice cream, and fish soup, using turtles taken from the nearby San Antonio River.

William Menger died at the hotel in 1871, at age forty-four, and Mary, assisted by her son Louis, ran the hotel for another ten years. Business boomed, especially with the arrival of the railroad in 1877; there was a convenient ticket office located off the lobby. During that time, Mary was San Antonio's largest employer, managing both the hotel and Western Brewery until closing it in 1878 at the urging of her teetotaler son. That's when Degen purchased the equipment and opened his own brewery nearby (see chapter 3).[41] Under Mary's watch, Western Brewery became the largest brewery in Texas.[42] She raised her children, supervised the ledgers, managed the purchasing, ran the kitchen, and did the book-keeping. She also made sure the hotel maintained its reputation as a first-class luxury hotel, installing gaslights and the equipment to manufacture their own gas in 1879, and purchased additional land so the enterprise could expand.

Until 1870, the US Army owned no land in San Antonio and had therefore decided to vacate the city. To keep the army stationed here, in 1867, the Mengers commissioned Kampmann to build a small ware-house between the hotel and the river, at the corner of Alamo Plaza, Crockett, and Lasoya Streets.[43] They leased this building to the army for two hundred dollars a month until Fort Sam Houston was completed in 1878.[44] The proximity of the beer garden to the army didn't hurt business, either. The brewery closed the same year the army moved out.

In 1881, Mary retired, selling the Menger Hotel to John Kampmann for $118,500. The sale included all land, buildings (including the old brewery and stables), imported French furnishings, fixtures, and cooking utensils, except those used by the family. He soon embarked on a complete overhaul, adding a new wing and lobby on the east, a third story on the original façade facing the plaza, and a three-story addition to the north replacing the brewery. The kitchen was relocated to better serve the increased capacity of the Colonial Dining Room. A laundry and additional private baths were added, and each room now had water piped in. The following year Kampmann added cottages at the rear for some of the staff, including a general headquarters for white women employees with separate small cottages for sleeping; the same was provided for white male staff. Black employees had a separate clubhouse for relaxation on-site but could not live on the grounds.[45]

The new east wing and lobby dwarfed the original hotel (see fig. 43). As his own client, Kampmann was planning and supervising construction this time, not laying stone. A visitor's guide to the city published in 1882 recommended the Menger as one of the best lodgings in the city. It was now the largest hotel in Western Texas, but the charges were moderate and the accommodations "common to first-class hotels in the large cities of the north."[46]

When Kampmann died, his son Hermann inherited the management of the hotel. In 1887, he further expanded the hotel, including a fourth floor on the southern side of the building and the famous Menger Bar facing Alamo Plaza, opening from both the street and the hotel. (It was relocated to the Crockett Street side in 1949.) The room was based on the House of Lords taproom in London and said to be an exact replica. Much of the $60,000 budget was spent on a solid cherry bar, which matched the cherrywood paneled ceiling.[47] The elegant interior included French beveled mirrors and gold-plated spittoons. It was in the Menger Bar that Teddy Roosevelt recruited volunteers for his "Rough Riders" in 1898 to fight in the Spanish-American War. Many a thirsty cowboy accepted Roosevelt's offer of a beer or two and found himself reporting for training the next morning at Fort Sam. In addition to hot rum toddies and ice cold drinks at the bar (using ice that was brought from Boston via Indianola and carted to San Antonio in custom-made insulated wagons), patrons could enjoy mint juleps in solid silver tumblers on the patio.[48] In 1889, Hermann oversaw another fifty-room addition, completed before his death in 1902. In 1909, the Kampmann Estate commissioned architect Alfred Giles (who had started his career in San Antonio working for Kampmann) to complete another addition on the south side of the building. He also altered the main façade, adding Renaissance Revival details utilizing modern materials, including cast iron and pressed metal and brick. He was also responsible for the redesign of the rotunda lobby space.[49]

There were more changes to come, including one in 1912 by Atlee Ayres, but by Prohibition, things were slowing down. The family was losing interest and divvying up shares among the heirs. In 1927, there was an announcement that the hotel would be torn down and replaced. The economic downturn of the Depression threatened demolition for the value of the land, which was to be used as a parking lot. The HABS documented and photographed the building for posterity, and J. Frank Dobie led a public campaign to save it.[50] Finally, in 1943, the Kampmann heirs sold it to W. L. Moody of Galveston for $205,000. Moody spent thousands more restoring and remodeling it, adding a new wing, and expanding it in time for HemisFair.[51] It was placed on the National Register of Historic Places in 1976–77 as part of the Alamo Plaza Historic District.

The Menger was Kampmann's most important project to date and helped establish his reputation as a builder and businessman. The hotel played an important role in San Antonio's cultural and social history. Captain Richard King of King Ranch stayed there so often that his favorite room was renamed the King Ranch Suite. It was there that he died in 1885, and the funeral was held in the lobby.[52] Other notable visitors over the years included Sam Houston, Sarah Bernhardt, Oscar Wilde, Lillie Langtry, Roy Rogers, and several presidents. Births and deaths, weddings, and the Battle of Flowers were all linked to the site. It even served as hospital rooms before the first hospital was built in the city.

In addition to notable guests, many important events took place there, including the organization on May 13, 1907, of the San Antonio section of the National Council of Jewish Women. It was and still is a favorite site for club meetings, birthday parties, wedding receptions, and other celebrations. The Menger has been expanded and altered to keep up with

Fig 43. The expanded Menger Hotel [Arthur W. Stewart, 1936, HABS TEX, 15-SANT, 10-18]

the times, but still reveals much of its history. It has been in continuous operation for over 150 years and retains its rank as one of the special places in the city.

The Mengers were also special people in the city's history. William served as alderman between 1857 and 1859. As captain of the Volunteer Fire Department Co. No. 1, he brought the first steam fire engine to San Antonio. During the cholera epidemic of 1869, he funded the building of the Santa Rosa Infirmary, which evolved into Christus Santa Rosa Medical Center.[53] Mary, in addition to running a profitable business, was active in St. Joseph's Church and Orphanage until her death at seventy-one. She contributed financially to the city's first Jewish synagogue and lobbied successfully to get a new post office built on Alamo Plaza.[54]

1868–71 St. Joseph's Catholic Church
623 E. Alameda [Commerce]

San Fernando Cathedral was the Catholic church for *all* San Antonians until 1855, when Bishop Odin, Bishop of Texas, founded St. Mary's Parish for Irish- and German-speaking Catholics, and the cathedral became the church for Spanish-speakers. Most of the German community in San Antonio was Catholic, including the Kampmanns at one time and the Mengers, and they petitioned for their own congregation. While the German-American community preferred to use one of the missions, either San José or Valero (the Alamo), the former was too costly and the latter was contracted to the government for use as military storage. Bishop J. M. Dubois purchased land on East Alameda [Commerce] Street, near the eastern town limits.

Gustave Friesleben was commissioned to draw plans for a German Gothic church, and John H. Kampmann was contracted to oversee the stonework. John Heitgen was named construction foreman.[55] Together they built a typical Bavarian church, which took thirty years to complete. Canvas covered the blank windows until the stained-glass windows imported from Munich were installed in 1902.

The cornerstone was laid November 5, 1868 (coinciding with San Antonio's 150th anniversary), the date inscribed in German on one side with the inscription, "See the house of God built by the people. Behold," and in Latin on the other side, "Habitation of God and Entrance to Heaven." The church was christened as St. Joseph in honor of San José Mission and the Virgin Mary's husband. Parishioners aided the construction team by donating money, physical labor, and the use of their own ox teams to haul stone from an east-side quarry (Pittman-Sullivan Park). They also gifted the church doors, windows, pews, altarpieces, and bells for the tower. Kampmann was paid $15,963.06 for building the shell: foundation, walls, and roof with an unfinished ceiling, and a fifty-foot base for a bell tower later named for Mary Menger, who contributed much of the money for its completion. In the German tradition, the four bells were also named, including one for Mary Menger.

The building, sans spire and only partially plastered, was completed in 1871 and celebrated by the entire city.[56] The procession stretched from St. Mary's to St. Joseph's, carrying a statue of their patron saint on their shoulders to its new home. The bells of St. Mary's and San Fernando rang, and homes along the route were festooned with flags and messages of welcome.

Theresa Gold noted that the fiftieth anniversary in 1918 was overshadowed by the anti-German sentiment of World War I, as was the seventy-fifth anniversary in 1943, due to World War II, dampening both celebrations. By the centennial in 1968, most Germans had moved out or been removed from the neighborhood for Hemis-Fair and had quit attending

Fig 44. St. Joseph's Catholic church before James Wahrenberger's spire was added [Witteman]

Fig 45. St. Joseph's Church surrounded by Joske's department store led to it being nicknamed "St. Joske's" [author]

St. Joseph's.[57] In 1945, Joske's Department Store, which was next door, offered to purchase the church and rectory so they could expand their store and parking lot. The parishioners voted unanimously to reject the offer, so Joske's expanded by building around the church, and the church was nicknamed "St. Joske's" (see fig. 45). The church outlasted the department store, which changed hands several times, and remains a vital part of the community. In 1947, ethnically assigned parishes were changed to geographical assignments, but many long-time members of St. Joseph's were given dispensation to continue their membership, and it still has a strong German identity.

1859/1873–75 St. Mark's Episcopal Church
315 E. Pecan St

Kampmann was also involved before and after the war in building one of the major Protestant churches in San Antonio, St. Mark's Episcopal Church on Pecan Street across from Travis Park. Today it stands as an expression of several different time periods and architects. It sits on what was originally part of the grounds of the Alamo that evolved into a nineteenth-century residential neighborhood. Even as stores and office buildings replaced the houses in the area, the church maintained its neighborhood feel, and it is still a strong presence in the area, serving a geographically expanded constituency. The most original parts of the building exhibit nineteenth-century attitudes toward both religion and Gothic Revival architecture. It also bears the scars of the Civil War, which interrupted construction.

Beginning in 1850, the first Protestant Episcopal mission in San Antonio was organized under Army Captain Rev. J. F. Fish, a post chaplain and member of the New York Ecclesiastical Society. A small group of the faithful, including Col. Dashiell, first met in an adobe building calling themselves Trinity Parish. Despite the fact that they were admitted to the diocese, the group floundered, and more than once they had to sell their assets to pay off debts. Construction of a building was actually begun in 1853 on Rincon [St. Mary's] Street, but, once again, the debts could not be paid. This time, the foundations laid by J. H. Kampmann were dug up and the materials sold.[58] Kampmann received a settlement check for his work in the amount of $1,000 in 1855.[59]

On Easter Sunday, April 16, 1858, Rev. Lucius H. Jones of Seguin again called believers to services. With the support of prominent citizens, including James Sweet and Mary Maverick, he was able to reorganize the congregation as St. Mark's Episcopal Church, and they were received into the Diocese of Texas. This time they met with success, perhaps because of a larger and wealthier membership. The city's population had increased from five thousand to seven thousand, including a large contingency of Eastern Anglos headquartered in San Antonio due to the recent Mexican War and the frontier conditions of Texas. Many career officers were Episcopalian, including Lt. Col. Robert E. Lee, who had supported the first efforts in 1850 and became a charter member of the new congregation in 1858.

Plans for the construction of a church began the same year. The land was donated by Vance Bros. and Samuel Maverick; Maverick's donation became Travis Park across the street. The edifice was designed by New York architect Richard Upjohn, who provided drawings for the building as well as comprehensive specs for its construction and detailing.[60] Kampmann again entered into a contract to provide materials and supervise construction. The limestone was drawn from a quarry on the site of the present zoo and Sunken Gardens, of which Kampmann was part owner.[61]

Upjohn was one of the foremost leading church architects in America in the mid-nineteenth-century, and this was his only work in Texas. He had no formal architectural education, but trained as a carpenter, cabinet maker, surveyor, and draftsman in England, where he grew up amid medieval Gothic architecture and in the Anglican church, and his appreciation of hand-craftsmanship was evident in the details of this church.

The cornerstone was laid December 22, 1859.[62] Once again, as at St. Joseph's, the parishioners were assisting, even laying stone. Ashlar stone walls built of locally quarried limestone supplied by Kampmann and laid in a random pattern outlined the simple basilican plan laid out by Upjohn. It was similar to other plans by Upjohn and consisted of a nave flanked by two side aisles, leading to a half transept and an apse behind the altar. The load-bearing walls were two feet four inches thick, exposed on the exterior and to be covered with a smooth white plaster finish on the interior.

Window and door surrounds had refined cut-stone sills and Gothic hood molds. The walls had reached approximately seven feet (half their intended height) when war broke out, and most of the principals involved in the building process were dispersed to fight—on both sides—leaving the building only partially done. Those called to the Confederacy included Sunday School teacher Lt. Col. Robert E. Lee, builder Col. Kampmann, Col. Albert Sidney Johnson, Maj. James Longstreet, and Lt. John Hood. Others remained loyal to the US Army, including Don Carlos Buell and D. H. Vinton, who served as Union generals. St. Mark's Parish organizer and Rector Lucius H. Jones volunteered as a Confederate chaplain and was killed in Louisiana.[63] The Bird's Eye map from 1873, the year construction resumed, shows the unfinished walls (see fig. 76).

The cream-colored stone turned gray—the demarcation line can still be discerned. The budding structure resembled the ruins of a Spanish mission, for which it was often mistaken in the 1860s. Construction resumed in 1873 under the leadership of Rev. Walter Raleigh Richardson, the new pastor who had arrived in 1868.[64] Kampmann resumed his involvement, as did General Robert E. Lee. In fact, the two became close friends, probably as a result of this project and their membership in the congregation. It took two more years to complete, and the first service was Easter 1875. Some sources indicate that the original plans were lost during the war and the building had to be finished from Kampmann's stonework, including the existing foundation.[65] The church was finally consecrated on St. Mark's Day, April 25, 1881, when the remaining building debt was finally paid off, three years after Upjohn's death.

It is unclear when or why Kampmann converted from Catholicism (if he did, in fact), but the family became staunch supporters of St. Mark's.[66] His separation from St. Joseph's may have been related to his membership in the Alamo Masonic Lodge or other aspects of his social and business community. St. Mark's membership roster contained many German names, including several of Kampmann's friends and clients. John and Caroline donated a stained-glass memorial window on the south side in thanks for her restoration to health after a severe and almost fatal illness. The window depicts Jesus and the Woman of Samaria flanked by large tablets with texts from the Evening Prayer: "Praise the Lord o my soul and forget not his benefits" on the left and "Who forgiveth all thy sin and healeth all thine infirmities" on the right (see fig. 50). There are also symbols of health throughout, such as the five-pointed star, an ancient symbol of health whose points represent the five members of the body in perfect health, and the Greek word *Ugeia* (health).

St. Mark's is considered an excellent example of medieval English True Gothic Revival. It is more architecturally and academically correct than most other Gothic Revival buildings, given Upjohn's training and philosophy. Capped with a castellated tower, the building featured low buttresses supporting the load-bearing walls at crucial points to allow more width for stained-glass windows, but it was not yet utilizing the High Gothic tradition of lofty flying buttresses. Quatrefoil designs and other Gothic details were seen repeated in the window tracery and hand-carved oak doors and in the mahogany pulpit. According to the HABS report, "in no other part of the country [could] be found any finer examples of hand carved woodwork as can be found in St. Mark's."[67]

The National Register Nomination cited the church's excellent and very early Texas example of nineteenth-century Gothic Revival: elaborate interior features, wooden trusses, octagonal wooden columns, and art-glass windows, all proceeding toward a chancel and altar area raised above the main floor.[68] Originally, the interior woodwork was to be milled in

Fig 46. The eastern end of St. Mark's showing the apse and belfry [Arthur W. Stewart, 1936, HABS TEX, 15-SANT, 8-3]

Fig 47 (top). St. Mark's view from southwest [Arthur W. Stewart, 1936, HABS TEX, 15-SANT, 8-1] Fig 48 (bottom). Stonework detail [Arthur W. Stewart, 1936, HABS TEX, 15-SANT, 8-4]

Fig 49. Nave and apse of St. Mark's [Joanna Valentine]

Fig 50. Caroline Kampmann's memorial window [Joanna Valentine]

New York (under Upjohn's supervision, probably) but it now fell to Kampmann's new planing mill.[69]

Richard Upjohn, a founder and president of the American Institute of Architects (AIA), was also involved in the Ecclesiological Movement. This was a reform movement within the Anglican Church that called for a return to more traditional medieval forms and the promotion of A.W.N. Pugin's English Gothic models as the only appropriate style for religious buildings. Upjohn "saw reform of church design as a means of improving both architecture and the practice of religion."[70] Ecclesiology held that architectural features must be inherently connected to church ritual—and vice versa. This required reform of both form and ritual. For example, building orientation should reflect the medieval rule of a western entry and an east-facing apse so that the congregants faced the rising sun, symbol of the resurrection and the beginnings of a new day. Steep roofs, lancet windows, and even the buttresses emphasized verticality, pointing heavenward. Ornament had to be liturgically correct. Upjohn's Trinity Church in New York (1839–46) demonstrated these qualities, as did St. Mark's on a smaller scale. All elements were adapted to the Texas climate, including louvered openings from the windowsills to the floor. These were fitted with a sash hung on pivots, so that from the outside the effect was that of deeply recessed paneling beneath the window, while the practical effect was to take advantage of cross breezes.

According to Charles Ramsdell, it was Dean Richardson, Rector of St. Mark's, who designed all the glowing memorial windows (including the Kampmann window) that gave the church warmth and color. He also stenciled with his own hand much of the ornamentation that was once on the walls and ceiling. He is even said to have designed the pulpit and laid out the landscaping.[71] The bell was cast from a canon found near the outer wall of the Alamo by Samuel A. Maverick but dated from an earlier altercation in 1813.[72] The inscription on the bell read in part, "I too have been born from works of death to words of life through Christ's eternal merit," referring to the Alamo and, perhaps, to the Civil War.[73]

There was a marked but coordinated contrast between the sanctuary's "exterior dominated by the power of the heavy limestone walls, [and] the interior['s] much lighter feeling conveyed by its timber framing."[74] The 100 x 56 foot interior sat six hundred and was visually divided between the apse (the sacred space) and nave, typical of Episcopal churches. This spatial progression was reinforced by the contrast of the plaster (originally stenciled) and the row of six columns separating the nave from the side aisles (see fig. 49). The columns were probably of a limestone core encased in cypress.[75] Forty-five-foot wooden arches sprang from the columns, which lifted the eye to the framework above: a network of Gothic arches, quatrefoils, and English trusswork. This wooden structure framed the raised altar; it was at this altar that Lyndon Baines and Lady Bird Johnson were married on November 17, 1934. Similar arches over the side aisles reached up twenty-five feet and were supported by flying buttresses three feet wide. Thus, the exterior and interior structures were independent of one another.

Later additions to the campus included the Parish Hall (1926) and Education Building (1927), both by Alfred Giles's successor firm with Albert Felix Beckmann (John Conrad's son), and additions and alterations to the sanctuary, including the narthex, bell tower, west end, and cloister (1948–49) by Henry Steinbomer. The Bethlehem Chapel (1951) was added immediately to the west of the Upjohn building, and in 1959, new organ components necessitated raising the sacristy roof. In 1962, St. Mark's was designated a Recorded Texas Historic Landmark, and in 1998, it was added to the National Register of Historic Places. In 2013, St. Mark's completed a $15 million overhaul and restoration begun fifteen years earlier, including a $2.6 million facelift to the sanctuary. The architectural firm of Ford, Powell & Carson restored much of the interior to more closely resemble the original, including bringing back the original plaster colors.[76]

1861–65 Civil War

These German-community buildings spanned the period of the Civil War, during which time Texas, San Antonio, and the German-American community were torn apart—it was often literally brother fighting against brother. While the delegates to the Texas Convention voted for secession 166 to 8, an examination of the popular vote for and against reveals a much closer separation (46,129–14,907). Within Bexar County, the vote was 827 for and 709 against.[77] Vereins and Texas Turners were split apart on issues of slavery, abolition, and secession, as was the larger German-American community. Many members of vereins resigned when the majority of the local organization voted the other way. The surviving organizations were generally those focused on gymnastics and education more than social and political issues. This was the contradiction of America. These were people who less than two decades prior had left Germany, the beloved motherland whose culture they never forsook, to secure personal freedoms and opportunities for their families. And many who enlisted on both sides were not in support of the issues but felt the need to support their community, social clubs, and friends. Like the rest of the United States, the community was torn asunder, and it survived the bitter rift, but at great cost.

Freethinkers have a long legacy in Germany, dating back to the early nineteenth century, when individuals were encouraged to think for themselves and not routinely accept what they were told by authority, which is what led many immigrants to come to Texas in the 1840s. Freethinking, however, could be interpreted two ways in the 1860s, with opposite results. One could either question social values and government as a theoretical entity and think for oneself, resulting in racial equality and the abolition of slavery, or question the federal government and vote for secession and the local authority of the Confederate States of America. Many German-Texas communities took the first path, especially in the Texas Hill Country and in Gillespie, Kerr, Kendall, Medina, and Bexar Counties. Some communities took a strong stand, forcing many to leave to avoid persecution under Confederate martial law. These included Sisterdale, Tusculum, and Comfort, which built the *Treue der Union* Monument to honor those citizens (mostly German) who resisted the Confederate cause. The monument, dedicated August 10, 1866, honors the conscientious objectors and Union soldiers from the surrounding area. The monument includes the family names of Kampmann friends and colleagues Berens, Degener, and Steves, and that of Peter Bonnet, age thirty. This was Caroline Bonnet Kampmann's brother who was wounded at the Battle of Rio Grande and died five months later, leaving a wife and two-year-old child. Three Bonnet brothers supported the Union cause, actively serving in uniform, and both Johann Carl (John Charles) and Heinrich (Henry) Daniel survived the war.

Conditions were different in the Hill Country than they were in neighboring San Antonio in the early 1860s. While the latter was directly under Confederate martial law, those living in neighboring areas were subject to "threat of annihilation by Confederate enforcers" with preemptive shoot-to-kill orders for resistance to the Cause.[78] San Antonians were exempt from this threat. The Kampmann family owned African-American slaves, as did 2 percent of the white population in Bexar County and 5 percent in San Antonio. As was the urban custom, most slaves were domestic servants. While Texas voted in favor of secession in 1861 by 76 percent, San Antonio defeated the motion 51 to 49 percent. Kampmann also voted to defeat it.[79] It is impossible to know why John and Caroline Kampmann chose their cause, and stood opposed to the Bonnet brothers, but it points out the difficult decisions faced by German-Americans in the 1860s. Kampmann chose to join the Confederate army as captain of Company B, a battalion of infantry made up of local German-Texans he had recruited, known as the German Company and part of the Texas Third Infantry under the command of Philip Noland Luckett.[80] War records indicate that on May 10, 1861,

> Col. Earl Van Dorn reported that a battalion of infantry had been raised in San Antonio, including Captain Kampmann—they captured a force of about 347 Union soldiers on the El Paso road without incident—they will be held as prisoners of war.[81]

His family biography records,

> At the outbreak of war, [Kampmann] raised a company of Germans, becoming Captain of a company that was attached to the Third Texas Infantry. They were stationed at Camp Verde for some time, and then ordered to Brownsville, where they served on frontier defense for about one year, then went to Galveston.[82]

1861 San Antonio Arsenal

S. Flores/Arsenal Streets

One of the first assignments given to the new captain in 1861 was to complete the arsenal begun by the US Army in San Antonio in 1859 and seized by the Confederacy on February 16, 1861. One of the oldest US military structures in Texas, the Texas Arsenal, was established as the permanent arsenal site for the Southern area by Jefferson Davis when he was US secretary of war in 1858. Captain R.H.K. Whitely selected a sixteen-acre site on the west bank of the San Antonio River that included a stretch of the San Pedro *acéquia*. Construction began in 1859, supervised by San Antonio building contractor John M. Campbell, whose brother W. W. Campbell received the stone contract.[83] Of the six to eight stone buildings called for in the plan for the arsenal, only two or three had begun when construction was halted in 1861, due to the outbreak of war. The most important and most expensive of the group was the Magazine, costing twenty thousand dollars.[84]

When General David E. Twiggs, US Commander of the Arsenal, surrendered it to the Confederate army in 1861, it became the San Antonio Arsenal. Kampmann replaced Campbell as the contractor for the building (and possibly the stone supplier). It was Kampmann who completed the barrel-vaulted ceiling of the limestone magazine structure and the roof. Wesley Shank's notes as part of the HABS documentation in 1968 said, "Cracks at the joint between vault and end walls indicate that the stones of the vault do not interlock with those of the end walls," indicating that Kampmann might only have done the vaulted roof.[85] The HABS drawings indicate the vault springline is at seven feet, three inches, slightly above the windowsill (see fig. 51). The stone changes color slightly at this point on the interior, but not on the exterior (see fig. 52 and 54). Thus it appears that Campbell built the outside walls, while Kampmann added the interior vault at a later date. This is supported by the date on the plaque over the entry (also above the springline), which says 1860. The plaque also contains a carving of a cannon, a pyramid of cannon balls, and a powder barrel.

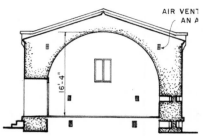

SECTION A-A

Fig 51 (left). San Antonio Arsenal Magazine plans [Charles. W. Barrow, Jr., 1968, HABS TEX, 15-SANT, 42E]

Fig 52 (below). San Antonio Arsenal Magazine [Dewey G. Mears, 1968, HABS TEX, 15-SANT, 42-E1]

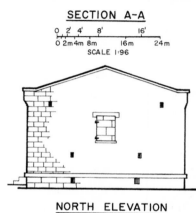

NORTH ELEVATION

The Magazine building was a long (30 x 110 feet) one-story rectangular structure with thick walls of ashlar limestone set on a limestone foundation. Stone blocks were twelve inches high, ranging in length from eighteen to thirty-six inches with coursed mortar set flush to make a smooth wall. The cream yellow soft stone was quarried locally,

Fig 53. Detail above western door [Dewey G. Mears, 1968, HABS TEX, 15-SANT, 42E--4]

showing occasional orange flecks and fossil shells.[86] "Details included end gables extending above the roofline, lintels protruding as hood molds, and the date carved in stone over the side entry."[87] It was referred to as Building 19 in the "San Antonio Arsenal Historical Report" requested by the Department of Defense in 1908, in which the author praised the Magazine's structure, saying,

> Its thick stone walls would have withstood almost any attack likely to have been made against it, with the field weapons of that era. This building was constructed with only two windows, both placed high for the protection of its occupants against gunfire from the outside, and to prevent its contents from being set afire by some blazing substance being thrown through a window.[88]

The interior was framed by the stone walls and vault. There were no ties or buttresses, and the white paint did little to hide the stoneworker's tool marks. "Carefully spaced vents and cavities in the walls permitted air circulation and reduced the danger of sparks igniting stored gunpowder. The arsenal supplied arms for south Texas and frontier defense, as well as for the Sibley expedition to New Mexico in 1862, and it was used throughout the war.[89]

According to the 1942 Department of Defense report, there were no extant files on the use of the Arsenal during the two years it was under control of the Confederacy, but according to Captain L. G. Gomolack,

Fig 54. Interior, San Antonio Arsenal Magazine [Dewey G. Mears, 1968, HABS TEX, 15-SANT, 42E-5]

the Arsenal was used for the production of Bowie knives and buckshot during the Civil War.[90] Two Confederate commanders led the post—Col. Sackfield Maelin (March 12, 1861–September 30, 1863) and Col. Philip Stockton (October 1, 1863–March 15, 1865).[91]

Following the war, the Arsenal was surrendered back to the US government on November 16, 1865, and renamed the US Arsenal in San Antonio.[92] Only the Magazine was in stable condition at the time of the surrender. The other buildings required substantial repairs, and the Arsenal was enlarged and finally completed in the early 1880s—not by Kampmann. It was deemed unsuitable for the military headquarters of Texas and the quartermaster's depot, so a new site was selected, but land acquisition and delays prevented the construction of Fort Sam Houston two-and-a-half miles northeast of Main Plaza until 1876.[93] The Arsenal then resumed use as the principal supply depot for frontier forts in the

Southwest and continued its use by the U.S. Army until being deactivated as an Arsenal and declared surplus war property in 1947.[94] The buildings were then utilized by various federal agencies for many years. H.E.B. Grocery acquired the eastern half of the property in 1981 and renovated it for use as their corporate headquarters.

During the Spanish-American War, the Arsenal manufactured saddles for Teddy Roosevelt's Rough Riders, and in 1914, it supplied General Pershing with weapons for his pursuit of Poncho Villa.[95] The Magazine played its most pivotal role following World War I, when it was used for storing leftover weapons and supplies, employing as many as 370. The Arsenal was an important fixture in one of the most active military cities in the United States.

Not much has been discovered about how Kampmann rose to the level of major, but from 1863 forward, war records refer to him as Major Kampmann. It was reported that on August 11 of that year,

> The Third Regiment of Texas refused to drill and obey orders evincing tumultuous and riotous evidences of insubordination— Kampmann was their commanding officer—deplorable discipline and lack of food seemed to be part of the cause.[96]

By 1864, his health required him to be reassigned to La Grange, where he supervised a factory in manufacturing Confederate hats for the duration of the war. This was probably the Alexander Hat Manufacturing Company, which produced Confederate powder, shoes, cotton bagging, leather, and rope, in addition to hats. At the beginning of the war, Texas had few factories, so the Confederacy had to quickly establish the manufacturing plants necessary to supply an army, or else import goods from Mexico. Hat factories scattered around the state produced military hats and blankets, employing local citizens as well as assigned soldiers. Most of these factories were destroyed after the war. According to the LaGrange *True Issue,*

> Maj. Kampmann is one of those go ahead kind of men, that works himself, and makes everything and everybody around, or under

his control do the same thing. The right man in the right place. We expect to be enabled to report an increased number of soldier's hats turned out from the manufactory in a short time. This factory delivered to the Clothing Bureau at Houston, between 1600 and 1700 hats during the month of October.[97]

Kampmann's biography concluded his war record,

[In Galveston, he] was promoted to Major, but his health was greatly impaired by rheumatism, and he was detailed to start a hat factory at La Grange, to make hats for the soldiers. Nearly every thing in the way of facilities and appropriate tools, etc., was lacking, but by employing mechanics [and machinery] from Mexico, he soon had the factory in good working order, and made thousands of hats which were turned over to Gen. Kirby Smith. He continued at that post till the end of the war.[98]

On February 14, 1866, Kampmann received a "full pardon and amnesty" signed by President Andrew Johnson "for all offenses by him committed, arising from participation, direct or implied, in the said rebellion," on the condition that he take the oath of loyalty, never own slaves or make use of slave labor, pay all costs, and not claim any property.[99] However, he continued to call himself Major Kampmann the rest of his life.

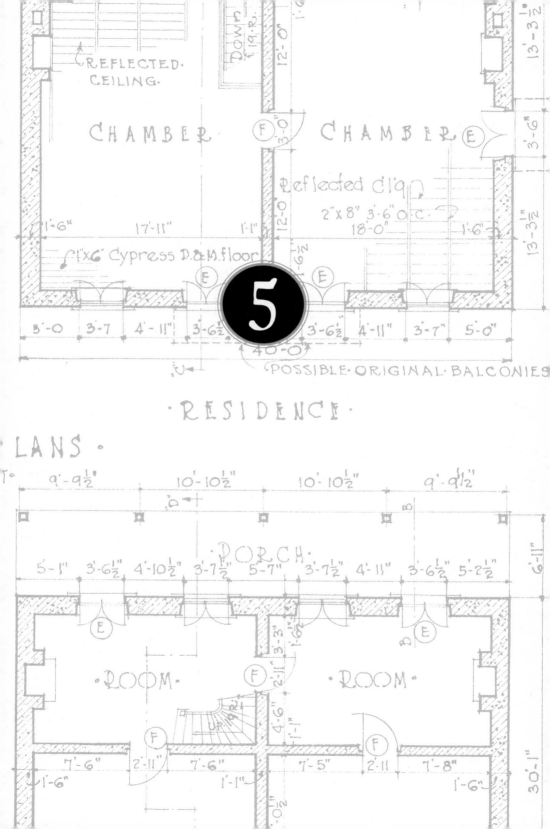

·REFLECTED·
CEILING.

CHAMBER

CHAMBER

Down
19'R.

12-0"

·REFLECTED· c'lg.

2"x8" 3'-6" O.C.

13'-3½"

3'-6"

13'-3½"

1'-6"

17'-11"

1'-1"

12-0"

18'-0"

1'-6"

1'x6" Cypress D.& M. floor

6½"

3'-0"

3'-7"

4'-11"

3'-6½"

3'-6½"

4'-11"

3'-7"

5'-0"

40'-0"

·POSSIBLE·ORIGINAL·BALCONIES·

·RESIDENCE·

PLANS·

9'-9½"

10'-10½"

10'-10½"

9'-9½"

·PORCH·

6'-11"

5'-1"

3'-6½"

4'-10½"

3'-7½"

5'-7"

3'-7½"

4'-11"

3'-6½"

5'-2½"

3'-3"

1'-6"

·ROOM·

·ROOM·

4'-6"

1'-1"

Up 19'R.

30'-1"

7'-6"

2'-11"

7'-6"

7'-5"

2'-11"

7'-8"

1'-6"

1'-1"

1'-6"

Reconstruction
1865-1880

—)•●•(—

Kampmann returned to his career in San Antonio with a title and a pardon, and used both to his advantage, implying loyalty to both sides. The buildings he was involved with for the next twenty years were mostly grand Victorian houses and businesses, the former as contractor, supplier, and occasional designer, and the latter as building materials supplier, investor, and, frequently, owner. What he had learned from managing the hat factory during the war was applied to his own business ventures now. A colleague later recalled, "Kampmann did all the contracting in those days. He specialized in erecting stone houses and later became owner of the Menger Hotel. His period of building extended between 1866 and 1888."[1]

Postwar clients included some of most well-known families in San Antonio (Groos, Halff, Oppenheimer, Steves), and their houses reflected the evolution of the pre-war single-story San Antonio German Vernacular to two-story American Victorian. The residences combined limestone masonry construction and foursquare plans with new decoration and details made popular by postwar taste and the need to mark a separation from the antebellum era, all made feasible by the Industrial Revolution. The arrival of the railroad in San Antonio in 1877 expanded the choices available and lowered the cost of building materials.

Kampmann finished his own home and built a Sash & Door Factory and office behind the house. By this time, he also owned or leased (either wholly or with an interest in) several stone quarries around San Antonio. He focused on the business side of the building industry and left the design to others, preferring the title "major" to "architect" in the advancement of his career. He also established himself as an entrepreneur and public servant, which is the subject of chapter 6.

ca 1870s Kampmann House and Planing Mill
Nacogdoches Street [demolished]

The first house Kampmann started working on when the war was over was his own home on Nacogdoches Street, making it into a showcase for his talents and industry.[2] From the front on Nacogdoches, it still resembled the other square symmetrical houses with a front parapet behind a full front porch over a raised basement. Surrounded by large yards on either side, it appeared much smaller than its final sixteen rooms would suggest. Postwar alterations included extending the front porch by one bay, and adding rooms to the front and a wide hall. Two new front rooms were the largest in the house, each with deep windows, broad fireplaces, and high hand-painted ceilings. A broad two-story back porch and stable were added, as well (see fig. 55).

The L-shaped house was limestone, stuccoed on the exterior and plastered on the interior. The plastering and interior work, including the hand-painted and plastered ceilings, were done by an Italian artisan brought over to this country by Kampmann (see fig. 56). The bathroom fixtures were crafted in Germany. The woodwork throughout was walnut, oak, cypress, and pine. It appeared to be a one-story house from the front, because the first-floor "basement" was camouflaged by the porch and the windows placed high on the wall (see fig. 57). But the space was never

Fig 55. John and Caroline Kampmann House, late 1860s. Compare with figure 10. The street was also widened in 1926, shortening the front yard. [Arthur W. Stewart, 1936, HABS TEX, 15-SANT, 19-1]

treated like a basement. The stairway leading from the main floor was carved walnut and finished with care, as was all the interior woodwork and flooring. Stained-glass windows and hand-stenciled floors of tongue-and-groove pine were indicative of the attention paid to detail. From the outside, the windows were only six inches above the ground, but on the inside, they were four feet, six inches above the floor, as the basement was of full height. The sills were native cypress, and the twelve-light, double-hung windows were milled in the East and shipped to Indianola, then brought to San Antonio by ox cart.[3] From the rear, however, the main house appeared to be two stories as the basement was fully revealed. The addition of a gabled ell enhanced this appearance.

The house was often described as a showplace of San Antonio. Zeven & Altmann's San Antonio Marble Works on E. Commerce Street advertised that they furnished both dressed and carved stone for the Kampmann residence; it was so well known in the city they could use it as a virtual billboard.[4] Even the new building in the rear, used as a stable and for storage of harnesses and carriages, and with a second-story bunkhouse, was carefully constructed and ornately decorated with lacy gingerbread under the cornice (see fig. 58). In fact, it was later used a residence by several descendants.[5]

Fig 56 (above). Stenciled ceiling [Arthur W. Stewart, 1936, HABS TEX, 15-SANT, 19-8]

Fig 57 (right). Stairs connecting main floor with basement [Arthur W. Stewart, 1936, HABS TEX, 15-SANT, 19-9]

Fig 58. Ornate stable and living quarters behind house [Arthur W. Stewart, 1936, HABS TEX, 15-SANT, 19-13]

In January 1872, the Kampmanns added a cast-iron fountain shipped from Philadelphia to their front yard (see fig. 59).[6] The eight- to ten-foot diameter fountain was described in the newspaper as a beautiful addition to his "palatial residence [. . .] emitting eight or ten streams likened to the branches of the weeping willow, [and] also one central jet that shoots up in a straight direction to the height of some twelve or fifteen feet."[7]

Decades later, the San Antonio *Express,* in describing the house, recalled:

> In these parlors and over-flowing to the broad porch was dispensed the hospitality which became widely known, during Civil War times and later when Generals Lee, Grant and Beauregard were entertained there at different times. It was at this period that the house, always renowned for the quality and variety of food served, became still more famous for a certain kind of mint-julep that Major Kampmann mixed himself from various ingredients imported from Europe and stored in the cool, dark shelves of his wine cellar.

Fig 59. Fountain added to front garden, shipped from Philadelphia, 1872; the cupola on the mill can be seen in the rear. [courtesy of Judith Carrington]

Certain elderly neighbors who remember back [. . .] still enjoy telling of seeing a julep party in progress in the hot afternoons, on the long front porch shaded with Marechal Neil roses and chinaberry trees. Other select parties were given in the old summer house, where coffee was served in the afternoon in accordance with customs brought from Europe.[8]

After Caroline's death in 1914, the main house sat empty. In 1926, it was converted into a clubhouse for "The Bright Shawl," a charity run by the San Antonio Chapter of the Junior League of America. Margaret Adams (married to John and Caroline's grandson, Ike Kampmann) was general chairman of the organization at the time. Rooms were converted into rest and reading rooms, a library, gift shop, and tea room, all needed due to the increasing Junior League membership. Alterations were to keep the charm of the old place, but make it functional for a new century.

The plans were to use the wide entrance hall with glass doors at both ends as a new circulating library with all modern features. The Spanish dining room, which could seat one hundred, was reserved for private parties. The large parlor on the left was chosen for the gift shop, and the parlor on the right, which included a private screened porch, was to be reserved as the Junior League clubroom. "Through the ground-glass doors at the end of the entrance hall is one of the most attractive features of this house—a large, irregularly shaped room with the western side all of old-fashioned simple stained glass windows, which will be used as a general lounge and reading room."⁹ The room to the right of the lounge was reserved for the housemother. The large bowed extension on the left of the house with hardwood cabinets and a private bath and dressing room was to be used as a restroom. The sunny room next to it became a sewing room for volunteers to repair donated garments for their supported charities. But it was the basement level they were most excited about:

Every visitor to this part of the house is escorted down another steep and mysterious short flight of stone steps into what was once the wine cellar, but which under the new regime will become the preserve closet. This one part of the lower floor will remain undisturbed, except that in place of cobwebbed wine and liquor bottles on the close-set shelves, there will be every variety of jellies and preserves from the pantries of Junior League members, to be offered for sale. In the rest of the lower floor, modernistic decorative ideas will run riot in exotic color and bizarre design. The lower hall and the former dining room on the right will be the main tea rooms, with quaint handmade furniture, painted in vivid colors, and copper Pastores lanterns with yellow glass sides. Wall brackets of wrought iron with yellow shades will add another colorful note.

In the long stone-flagged, flower-draped passage which stretches the full width of the house, under the front porch a conservatory annex to the regular tea-rooms will be arranged, with growing plants as the chief decorative feature, and wrought iron tables and chairs from the boulevards of Southern Europe for furnishings. Public entrance to the basement floor will be through this passage, and the sign of "The Bright Shawl" painted to represent a Chinese shawl will be hung at the south steps.[10] The stable was rechristened "The Loft," with two immense rooms to be used as studio spaces for sculptors and painters.

Fig 60. Entrance to wine cellar in basement [Arthur W. Stewart, 1936, HABS TEX, 15-SANT, 19-11]

The plan was to use the proceeds from this venture to establish a children's hospital/ baby clinic to be administered through the adjacent First Presbyterian Church Children's Free Clinic Plan, a program close to several generations of Kampmann women, beginning with Caroline. The Bright Shawl was a huge success and soon outgrew their accommodations. Three years after they moved in, they sponsored a fundraiser in conjunction with the opening of the new Majestic Theatre, at which they raised the $30,000 necessary to move to a new location. Their new home at 819 Augusta Street was a limestone rock house designed by Alfred Giles. Less than ten years later, the Kampmann House was bulldozed and the site used as a parking lot for the First Presbyterian Church.

Kampmann Planing Mill

Elm Street between Fifth and Nacogdoches
Streets [demolished]

Kampmann's postwar focus was on re-establishing his home as a social center and his reputation as a businessman in the building industry and in the city. In the 1870s, he began running ads in the local paper announcing his new steam-powered factory and his ability "to contract for all kinds of mason work, stone cutting, carpenter work, plastering, and painting."[11] In October 1878, he obtained a building permit to enlarge his factory. What started as a workshop for the completion of his own home became the Kampmann Planing Mill located at Fifth and Elm Streets next to his house along the *acéquia* (see fig. 61). He received his first load of lumber delivered to the new Sunset Railroad Station on February 15, 1877.[12] That year he added an office between the house and the mill, "with a most attractive and imposing cornice, imported from St Louis."[13] This was probably the building referred to as the "stable" seen in figure 58, which was later used as a residence by John Bennett and Florence Herff.

The Sanborn Map Company, founded in 1867, published maps to aid insurance companies in determining potential fire risks. They

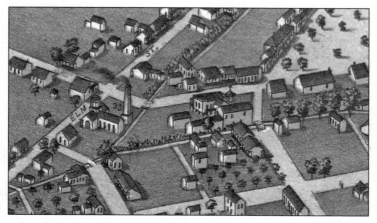

Fig 61. Kampmann's Planing Mill (#33) is across the acequia from his house. Kampmann built several other houses in this neighborhood. [Koch 1873]

were updated continually and contained valuable information about the use, size, shape, materials, heights, and functions of buildings in urban areas. They identified the location of doors and windows and other pertinent information, such as the location of flammable materials or equipment. For riskier buildings, including lumber yards, they could be quite detailed. The 1888 Sanborn Map includes the following information about his factory: it was located in a residential neighborhood of many wooden structures; there was an office and two sleeping rooms on site in addition to lumber sheds and wooden storage buildings; and there was no watchman on duty. The factory equipment included planers, woodworkers, saws, sanders, a gas engine, forge, mold makers, sharpeners, turning lathe, heater, and a fifty-horsepower boiler with a trestle tank.

Fig 62. Kampmann Planing Mill [courtesy of Judith Carrington]

The main structure of the factory was twenty by seventy-five feet, with an addition that measured thirty by seventy feet. The tall smokestack of his successful business was a neighborhood landmark, especially when the whistle blew every day except Sundays and could be heard all over town at seven a.m., noon, one p.m., and six p.m.[14] His employees (starting with 5 and eventually numbering 150 men) included planers, woodworkers, molders, and shapers.[15] The City Directory of 1877–78 identified Kampmann as architect and builder and listed his services as "building, contracting, dealing in lumber laths, shingles, building stone and material, plastering, painting, woodwork, rock sawing, manufacturing doors, sashes and blinds" (see fig. 63).[16] The blind and sash businesses became popular and necessary after the Industrial Revolution. It was much cheaper, more efficient, and more cost-effective to utilize mass-produced, pre-fabricated, standardized, machine-made pieces, such as windows, mantels, and even whole staircases, than to hire carpenters to make each piece individually, by hand and on-site. What had become a symbol of wealth because of its demanding labor costs was now affordable en masse.

Millwork was defined as:

> finished woodwork used in buildings that has been prepared in a woodworking shop or mill where machinery is used as far as possible in its manufacturing. It comprises doors, sash windows, transoms, frames, trim, moldings, stairs, columns, paneling, and built-in cabinets. For the most part these are built in a shop and sent to the job where trim carpenters install them. Millwork is not siding, clapboards, flooring, framing lumber, veneers, lath or shingles.[17]

Blinds were originally part of the name of most millwork companies, like Kampmann's, but they went out of vogue after 1900, replaced by screens, awnings, and air-conditioning.[18] Planing mills took rough lumber and made it into finished products. The planer dressed the wood and patterned it into different pre-defined stocks. There were a large number of national companies, most located near forests in Minnesota, Wisconsin,

Fig 63. John Kampmann's ad [1877-78 San Antonio City Directory]

and Michigan. There were also local companies specializing in Texas mesquite and cedar as well as Louisiana pines, for example. In San Antonio, there were a number of similar businesses by the end of the nineteenth century.

Kampmann hired both his son Gus and his nephews Charles and Joseph Boelhauwe (Gus's cousins) to help out, hoping they would eventually succeed him in the running of the business. Gus dropped in and out, adding and dissolving partnerships, and eventually opted out entirely, leaving it to Charles G. Boelhauwe, who continued to operate the company under his own name for many years (see fig. 64–65).[19]

1873 Friedrich and Gertrude Groos House
318 E. Alameda [Commerce] St. (demolished 1967)

Friedrich Wilhelm (1827–1912), Karl (Carl) (1830–1892), and Gustav (1832–1895) Groos immigrated from Germany with their widower father

Fig 64 (top). Gus Kampmann's ad [1883-84 San Antonio City Directory] Fig 65 (bottom). Drawing of Charles G. Boelhauwe's Mill [Morrison, 1890: 99]

Karl Wilhelm Groos and five brothers and sisters (Julie, Emilie, Adolph, Hedwig, Wilhelmine) in 1848. The family settled in Latium, one of the German intellectual communities. Friedrich came to San Antonio two years later to work with the mercantile firm Guilbeau and Callaghan, eventually becoming a partner, and went to Eagle Pass to represent the firm there. His brothers joined him in Eagle Pass, and in 1854, following Callaghan's death, they opened their own general merchandise and freighting business, F.

Fig 66. The Brothers Groos
[San Antonio Light]

Groos and Company, with branches in San Antonio, New Braunfels, and Matamoros.

In small towns, especially on the frontier, merchants frequently added a small banking enterprise to their businesses as a convenience to their customers and to provide currency exchange services for traders and freighters in border towns. When the firm F. Groos & Company moved to San Antonio in 1866, the bank was increasingly the focus of the business, and the mercantile and freighting businesses were abandoned entirely by 1874. Kampmann's protégé Alfred Giles designed a new building at Commerce Street and Groos Alley [Navarro Street] in 1879, the first structure in San Antonio built specifically to serve as a bank.[20] The private F. Groos & Company became Groos National Bank in 1912.[21] Friedrich, Carl, and Gustav all worked with Kampmann in building suitable residences within a few blocks of each other that expressed their new status as successful bankers and prominent leaders in San Antonio: Friedrich in 1873, Carl in 1880, and Gustav in 1875.

Friedrich Groos was educated in Germany as an architectural and civil engineer. He spent the war years in Monterrey, Mexico, with his family, returning to San Antonio in 1866. He was well acquainted with Kampmann, having served as president of the German-English School for twenty years and president of the Casino Club. He was elected for three terms as city alderman while W.C.A. Thielepape (also a member of the Casino Club) was mayor. Groos commissioned Thielepape, who had designed the Comal County Courthouse and may have worked on the design of Casino Hall, to design a substantial house on Avenida de la Alameda [Commerce St.] across the street from St. Joseph's Church. Kampmann was the contractor.

The two-story Neoclassical house had a symmetrical three-part façade, the center portion projecting forward into a square entry portico, featuring a grand entry. Above the porch was a balcony entered from a large French window flanked by two equally tall set windows. Between the windows and the door were four tall pilasters supporting an entablature and a shallow pediment. On either side of the central projection were two tall shuttered double-hung windows on each floor, framed by stone sills and lintels. A stringcourse ran across the front at the balcony level between the quoined corners of the house (see fig. 67).

Although the front of the house was covered with stucco, the coursed limestone base was visible on the other three sides. The house was fifty-four by forty-three feet deep with an extension on one side that measured another forty feet back, making an L-shape with an extended gallery on both floors. Friedrich and Gertrude Rodriguez Groos needed a big house for their large family. They lived in San Antonio for seven years before the house was completed, but she died in December of that same year, leaving him with eight children; he married Anna Siemering the following year, and they had eight more children. The huge two-story house was "grand in concept and magnificent in detail with inlaid floors, graceful winding stairways, and a commanding balcony overlooking the portico."[22] Granddaughter Tulitas Jamieson recalled "frequently going to the big house, built of yellowish Texas granite. [. . .] A huge affair, the entrance hall being big enough to hold a dance in."[23]

Anna died in 1911; her husband Friedrich in 1912. The house was acquired by St. Joseph's Catholic Church, and in 1929 it became the

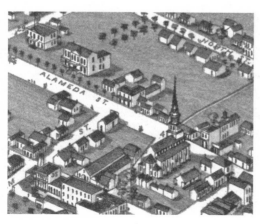

Fig 67. Koch's Bird's Eye Map shows the Friedrich and Gertrude Gross house above the m in Alameda Street. St. Joseph's church, which later acquired the house, is #4 on the map. [Koch, 1886]

headquarters for St. Joseph's Benevolent Association for nearly forty years. In the mid-1960s, it was part of the parcel to be razed for Hemis-Fair. There was much discussion about saving the house and moving it to another site, but the cost was thought to be prohibitive. The house was dismantled and the stones numbered with hopes of rebuilding it in La Villita, but that never happened; the stones may have ended up in one of the walls surrounding La Villita. Lewis Fisher's eulogy for the house read, "But the numbered stone blocks [. . .] did not rise from their heap to be reassembled. After many were found to be broken or missing, there seemed nothing to do but haul the rest away."[24]

King William

The other two Groos brothers, Gustav and Carl, built nearby in the King William neighborhood. This neighborhood was the first planned suburb of San Antonio, built on land that once belonged to the Alamo mission. When the mission was secularized in 1793, the farmland was surveyed by Pedro Huizar and split among Indian and other families living there, and ex-soldiers who petitioned the Spanish government. Huizar and Vicente Amador, charged with dividing the land, were also given land grants for their efforts. These last two grants became the basis for the King William neighborhood, subdivided and sold to developers, then settled by Germans in the 1850s. By the 1870s, there were a few houses scattered throughout the area, but still plenty of farmland. The streets were shaped by the contours of the river, and the neighborhood took on the name of one of the prominent streets, Kaiser Wilhelm Strasse. During World War I, the street was given the patriotic name Pershing Street in order to counter the anti-German sentiment. Following the war the old name was Anglicized into King William. At first the lots were fairly large, demanding grand houses, which were supplied by successful German American businessmen. Lots were further subdivided, and the infill of small vernacular Victorian houses (such as the Joseph Ball House, built by Kampmann in

1860) created an eclectic neighborhood in terms of house size and style. Kampmann built at least a handful of these grand houses in the 1870s, most notably the Carl Groos and Edward Steves Houses.

Alfred Giles (1853–1920) also designed a number of houses in King William, both with Kampmann and separately. Giles was educated in England and apprenticed to an architectural firm there. He arrived in Texas in 1873. Giles worked as an apprentice in Kampmann's office for three years, learning stone masonry and woodworking, before establishing his own firm in 1876 and becoming one of San Antonio's most prominent architects.[25]

ca 1875 Gustav and Anna Groos House
231 Washington

Gustav and Carl selected prime sites, the former on Washington St. on the river and the latter on King William Street, a few blocks away. In 1875, Kampmann prepared a proposal and estimate for building Gustav's house. While it was smaller than either of his brothers' homes, it was no less grand; the estimate was almost $11,000. The rectangular single-story house had limestone walls one and a half feet thick. The doors were made from Louisiana cypress and the specs included good-quality tin for the roof. Interior walls were plastered and whitewashed over the limestone. Windows were tall in the German fashion, framed by shutters and stone lintels and sills. A three-bay porch was centered in the front, decorated with gingerbread lace and scrollwork, forming a Victorian Gothic arch shape. The scrollwork might have come from Kampmann's mill. Above the arch was a shallow gable (see fig. 68).

It was nearly identical in plan to Friedrich's house but smaller; they only had eight children. The twenty-one-hundred-square-foot building contained six rooms—hall, parlor, dining room, master bedroom, and two additional smaller bedrooms for the children. There was also an extension in the back containing the kitchen and an additional bedroom,

Fig 68. Gustav and Anna Groos House [author]

possibly a servant's room. No architect has been identified, and it is possibly that Thielepape's plans for Friedrich's house were merely simplified by Kampmann. Like that house, stone steps approached the entry, which boasted grand double doors of cypress and impressive interiors with great attention to detail.

1874–77 Edward and Johanna Steves House
509 King William St.

The Steves House, begun in 1874 and finished in 1877, helped establish the reputation of Alfred Giles, recently arrived from England and employed by John H. Kampmann. It was he who taught Giles how to work with native Texas limestone. Kampmann oversaw construction of the house and probably provided the limestone quarried at the head of the river, and it was he who hired Anthony Earhart as chief mason on the job. Giles's role is not clear, but it is presumed he drew plans for the house. The house reflects both Giles's and Kampmann's styles (see fig. 69–70).

Edward Steves (1829–1890) immigrated from Germany to Texas with his family in 1848, first settling in New Braunfels, where he learned the skill of cabinetmaking. After marrying Johanna Kloepper in 1857, the family lived near Comfort, Edward splitting his time between carpentry in San Antonio and farming in the Hill Country. They moved to San Antonio in 1866 with their three sons and became prominent in the business community and German society. Steves and Kampmann were close friends, working together in public affairs and as members of the same clubs. Steves established a lumber business, specializing in imported woods brought by ox cart and then railroad, later becoming a competitor of Kampmann's Planing Mill with Steves Sash and Door Company. Like Kampmann, he invested in real estate and became one of the wealthiest men in San Antonio. Steves Lumber Company later became Steves & Sons.

Fig 69. Edward and Johanna Steves House [author]

Fig 70. The intricate woodwork decoration added a Victorian delicacy to the façade and shows the evolution of Kampmann's plain German-Texas style into a Victorian mansion by icing the basic stone house with gingerbread trim. [Jack Boucher, 1961, HABS TEX, 15-SANT, 25-2]

The house had a good symmetrical German base that transitioned into a substantial Victorian Renaissance Revival house, capped with a French mansard roof. It also had small Gothic touches, such as the sudden asymmetry in plan and the quatrefoils, pendils, and other decorative details. Slender cast-iron columns divided the five-bay porch that ran the width of the fifty-foot front façade and created a balcony on the second level. The limestone façade of earlier German vernacular houses was made fancier here by the use of ashlar stone instead of rough- cut randomly laid stone. The five windows on each of the first two floors were arched instead of square. A mansard roof capped the eclectic façade, highlighting the delicate shingle patterns, window surrounds, Italianate brackets, and cast-iron cresting. All the ornamental details, including the geometric shingles on the attic, the gingerbread on the porch, and the eave brackets, as well as the spindles and pendils on the balcony, displayed the work of the sawmill, whether it was Kampmann's, Steves's, or one in the East (see fig. 70). In addition, there were handsome hand-crafted details. The overall effect of the details gave the upper part of the house a more French flavor than German.

The three-story mansion was completed in three years, at a cost of $15,000. Mary Carolyn George described it as "the most famous landmark of the Victorian period in San Antonio [and] the jewel of King William Street, [. . .] which is virtually a museum of late nineteenth-century architecture."[26] It was surrounded by a pegged-and-tenoned wooden fence.

At first glance, the house was a classic four-room hall and parlor plan with tall ceilings and expansive windows that circulate air crosswise. But the L-shape plan of the house belied its foursquare appearance. Thirteen-inch-thick limestone walls aided in regulating indoor temperatures. Interior shutters kept the exterior façades clean, and with sliding doors, allowed rooms to be shut off from light or visitors. A central hallway provided cross-ventilation from front to back and contained a beautiful hardwood staircase. Imported mahogany and native walnut were used throughout the house. To the left of the stairs were a sitting room and formal dining room, to which a conservatory and kitchen were added. On the other side of the hallway were another

Fig 71. Side view shows Johanna's Victorian conservatory for cultivating plants and serving breakfast or tea. The bottom floors look like Kampmann's typical grand house while the Second Empire attic looks more like Giles's work [Jack Boucher, 1961, HABS TEX, 15-SANT, 25-3]

parlor and office, all with thirteen-foot ceilings. Upstairs were four bedrooms, and the third-floor attic gave the family a party room and plenty of play space.

The house was situated on a corner, making the informal asymmetrical rear façade visible from the side street. The two-story frame and stone carriage house was built at the same time as the house. Two buildings were later added at the back of the lot—the servants' quarters and garage—as well as a thirty-six-by-seventy-five foot brick-lined natatorium built in 1913, fed by an artesian well. This was the first indoor swimming pool in the city and was used daily by Johanna Steves. The prominent fountain in the lavishly landscaped front yard was, like Kampmann's fountain, a souvenir from the 1876 Philadelphia Centennial Exposition.

Edward and Johanna raised three sons in the house. He died in 1890,

Fig 72 (left). Central hallway with grand staircase [Jack Boucher, 1961, HABS TEX, 15-SANT, 25-6]

Fig 73 (right). Etched-glass pocket door separating sitting room from dining room [Jack Boucher, 1961, HABS TEX, 15-SANT, 25-7]

while she and her youngest son Ernest lived there until their deaths in 1930. For the next two decades, the house was partitioned and rooms rented. In 1952, granddaughter Edna Steves Vaughan and husband Curtis donated the house to the SACS in honor of her grandparents, Edward and Johanna, and parents, Albert and Fanny Baetz Steves. It has been carefully restored as a house museum, designated a Texas Historic Landmark, and placed on the National Register of Historic Places.

1875/8 Solomon and Fannie Halff House
142 Goliad

Brothers Mayer (1836–1905) and Solomon (1838–1905) Halff were partners in the mercantile business and pioneers in the Texas cattle ranching industry. They were from a Jewish family in the Alsace region of France and came from many generations of livestock traders who followed strict Jewish laws for butchering.[27] The Halffs were suffering from the poor economy and political events in Europe at mid-century, so Mayer left for America, as did his cousins. Solomon followed in 1857, at the age of nineteen, to work as a bookkeeper in what was becoming an extended-family dry-goods business. Mayer began accepting produce and cattle as payment and expanded the business to include groceries.

During the Civil War, the brothers ran into political troubles, including the threat of Mayer's conscription into the Confederate army and Solomon's draft into the French army. They left that area; laid low for a while; and in 1864, moved to San Antonio and established a dry goods business with Abraham Levy (husband of the Halff's cousin Esther). In 1872, they separated from Levy and established M Halff & Bro., Wholesale Dry Goods, located on Commerce Street; they also opened a branch in New York. They began trading in wool and "were hailed as 'wool kings' in San Antonio, the city known as the 'wool market' of the world."[28] Throughout their partnership, Solomon managed the store and went on buying trips, while Mayer attended to their expanding cattle business. The partnership acquired land, eventually over a million acres in West and South Texas, on which they ran cattle. Solomon got increasingly involved in the cattle end of the business, breeding cattle and running cattle drives.

Eventually, they added banking to their services. Solomon gradually became more active in the banking enterprise, and the brothers drifted apart professionally, especially after Mayer became involved in a competing bank, the City National Bank. Solomon responded by getting involved in a competing dry goods firm. By the turn of the century, the partnership had dissolved, but both brothers remained active in San Antonio religious and social life. They were both founding members of Temple Beth-El and general patrons of the arts in the city—and they lived across the street from one another behind the Eagar House in the German neighborhood later developed into HemisFair Park. Solomon became chairman of the board and vice-president of Alamo National Bank, while Mayer thrived in the cattle business.

Fig 74. Solomon Halff House [author]

In 1871, John Kampmann had purchased a lot on Goliad Street, which was part of the original Domingo Diego Acosta grant. He built a house on the property in 1875, which he sold to Nathan Halff in 1877. By 1879, Solomon Halff acquired it, and he and his wife, Fannie Levi, and their five children were the first residents of the house.[29] The two-story, L-shaped, wood-and-limestone house featured a front porch with a second-floor balcony, both outlined with machined dentils and brackets in the Victorian tradition. The intersecting gable roofs were supported by Italianate brackets (see fig. 74).

Solomon died in May 1905, eulogized in the newspaper as "a promoter of all progression in this city" and a man "highly esteemed for that very fortunate gift of nature—kindness."[30] Mayer died nine months later. Both were buried in Temple Beth-El Cemetery. Solomon's house was divided into a boarding house for two decades, and both houses were saved from demolition during the urban renewal efforts for HemisFair, becoming temporary pavilions. Mayer's grand 1893 Moorish house (designed by Alfred Giles) was the Falstaff Beer Garden, while Solomon's Victorian Gothic was a French restaurant called Maison Blanche. After the fair, Solomon's house served as the office of Dr. Arleigh Templeton, first president of the University of Texas at San Antonio, while the new campus was being built.

1878 Daniel and Louise Oppenheimer House
Jefferson and Pecan Streets [demolished]

The Oppenheimer brothers were also descendants of generations of kosher butchers in France. At age seventeen, Daniel Oppenheimer (1839–1915) left Bavaria for Texas. He soon sent for his brother, Anton, and together they ran D. and A. Oppenheimer, Wholesale Dry Goods, a retail and grocery store in Rusk, Texas, adding banking services in 1858. Business was interrupted by the Civil War, in which Daniel served as a Confederate colonel. Although the brothers opposed slavery, they served out of loyalty to the state of Texas.[31] After the war, the brothers moved their business to San Antonio, opening a store at Commerce and Soledad Streets. They expanded their interests into ranching, land speculation, and banking, culminating in the D & A Oppenheimer Bank.

Daniel married Louise Goldstein in 1869, and in 1875, they purchased land adjacent to Travis Park at the corner of Jefferson and Pecan

Fig 75. (top) The opulent Daniel and Louise Oppenheimer House, ca. 1936. When it was demolished, the materials were carefully salvaged and used in another house. [Florence Collett Ayres 83-648 UTSA SC]

Fig 76 (left). The partially completed St. Mark's can be seen at the bottom. Kitty-corner to that is the elaborate Oppenheimer House. Behind it on the opposite corner of the block is the Rhodius House, and just up from that at #24 is Fire Station #2. The site of the Alomo Literary Club is at #12. [Koch 1873]

Streets across from St. Mark's Church for $2,500 in gold from the Maverick family. They hired Kampmann to design and build the house on Jefferson St., where they raised seven children.[32] The design of the two-story L-shaped rock house was similar to that of the Solomon and Fannie Halff House being built at the same time. According to the San Antonio *Express*, the house was "constructed from plans made by W.S. Walters, Esq., who has proved himself master of his profession and whom Maj. Kampmann constantly employs, on account of his very extensive business."[33] A retraction printed the next day stated that

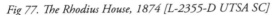

Fig 77. The Rhodius House, 1874 [L-2355-D UTSA SC]

Maj. Kampmann was the architect who drew out the plans. The paper continued their praise:

> The building is gotten up first class in every respect, with all modern improvements, including gas and water and in fact everything that taste can suggest and money procure. The wood work in the entire house is furnished in the finest manner, whilst the front doors are really a work of art, being made of solid walnut, beautifully carved and polished, one would think in a manner more suited to the finest wardrobe than to an outside door. The doors were made and finished by Mr. S.M. Bullard, who, as a workman in this line, has no equal in Texas, if in the South. Mr. Kampmann is indeed to be congratulated on securing Mr. Bullard's services. [. . .] [The building] is one of the finest of the fine buildings put up by this gentleman, and will certainly be a monument to his business qualifications as one of the foremost architects and builders of Western Texas.[34]

On the opposite corner of the block at Avenue C [Broadway] and Travis behind the Beth-El Synagogue was the house that Kampmann built for Christopher Rhodius in 1874, designed by Friesleben. The twist here was breaking the façade to address the corner and, again, applying Victorian gingerbread trim and an attic that looked out in several directions (see fig. 77).

Kampmann Family Houses

Between 1875 and 1881, Kampmann's three surviving children married, and their father aided them in securing homes to various degrees. When Eda (1855–1925) married John Herff (1850–1882) in 1875, Kampmann deeded them a lot and house on Losoya Street between Houston and Commerce near the Commerce Street Bridge "for and in consideration of the love and affection which I have for my daughter Eda Kampmann Herff and her husband John Herff."[35] Kampmann had long been acquiring property by this time, and it is unclear whether the house occupied by the newlyweds was the existing house or one rebuilt by Kampmann. The house can be seen in Koch's Bird's Eye Maps of 1873 and 1886, but was demolished between 1887 and 1892.

John was the prominent doctor son of Dr. Ferdinand Herff, noted Freethinker, early San Antonio settler, and medical pioneer—and one of Kampmann's first clients. John and Eda's house was considered a showcase of San Antonio graciousness, a large decorated two-story version of the square German American house suitable for a prominent family. When John died less than a decade later at age thirty-two, Eda and her children moved in with her parents; she later remarried.

Herman Kampmann married Lizzie Simpson in 1880, and they moved into an ornate house on Avenue E and 4th Street on property owned by Kampmann. It seems likely that Kampmann also oversaw construction and supplied materials for this grand two-story house, as it followed the familiar four-bay Greek Revival Kampmann pattern with a bowed shape on the side. Like the two Herff Houses, it was two stories instead of one. At some point, it was remodeled by Coughlin and Ayres. According to an article in the San Antonio *Express*,

> While [the old Herman Kampmann house] was under construction, a strolling Italian stone cutter came into San Antonio and applied for and secured the contract to do the carving at the entrance. The result was an extraordinarily beautiful and intricate piece of carving. With his work completed, the stranger shouldered his pack and departed and today his name is unknown but his labors have lived as another example of the artist unrewarded.[36]

After Elizabeth Simpson Kampmann's death in 1916, the building briefly served as the Salvation Army citadel. Son Ike S. Kampmann, attorney for his mother's estate, sold the property to the Bexar County Lodge of Perfection for $65,000.[37] The house was demolished in 1920 and replaced by the Scottish Rite Masonic Cathedral.[38] But the ornately carved stonework, entry lintel, and windows were saved and incorporated into the new house being built by Henry T. Phelps for Ike S. Kampmann, Jr. (he was

Fig 78. Materials from Hermann and Lizzie Kampmann's house were recycled into their grandson Ike Kampmann's house in the 1920s [Jason Rodriguez]

a contractor and Herman's grandson and John's great-grandson), as were the bay windows, floors, cabinets, and gazebo (see fig 78).[39] This house, incidentally, was located on land originally acquired by John and Caroline Kampmann and known colloquially as "Mrs. Kampmann's goat pasture," later as Laurel Heights, and then Monte Vista.

Youngest son Gus Kampmann married Emily Elmendorf in 1881, and they moved into a house probably paid for by Kampmann. "Henry Pauly has secured the stone work from Major Kampmann for the residence of the Major's son Gus. Henry considers this quite a compliment, Major Kampmann being probably the oldest and best-known builder in western Texas."[40] Pauly also worked on the Menger Hotel additions for Kampmann.

1880–84 Carl and Hulda Groos House
335 King William

Kampmann's final house project was a house built for Carl Groos (1830–1893) in collaboration once again with Alfred Giles, Giles as designer and

Fig 79 (top). Detail; this was the last house built by John H. Kampmann [author]

Fig 80 (left). Carl and Hulda Groos House [author]

Kampmann as contractor. This elegant house on King William took three-and-a-half years to complete and is similar in many ways to the houses built by Kampmann for Groos's brothers and Edward Steves nearby.

It was a two-story square limestone block with bumpouts on either side to bring in more light and create spacious interiors. The symmetrical façade featured a beautiful front door flanked by tall, shuttered, double-hung windows framed in stone, and protected by a porch that extended across the façade. Above the porch was a gallery, repeating the symmetrical arrangement of windows and including a projection that sheltered the steps leading to the front door. Both the porch and the gallery were adorned with thin cast-iron columns and delicate trim that contrasted Gothic trefoils with Art Nouveau whiplashes (see fig. 79). The walls were a smooth ashlar stone with a regular cut, and the façades were given further definition by beveled corner quoins raised slightly from the wall surface. The windows and doors were emphasized by deep reveals into the thick rock that provided insulation. The slate roof was crowned by an Italianate belvedere surrounded by a cast-iron balustrade.

As in the Steves House, the entry hall was dominated by a massive central staircase built of mahogany, which led up to the bedrooms and eventually spiraled to the belvedere. The hall separated a parlor and music room on the left from a sitting room, library, grand dining room with butler's pantry, and a kitchen on the right. The house featured mahogany and walnut throughout, as well as inlaid pecan and walnut striped and parquet floors bordered with fretwork, all hand done, and stained-glass windows. Light fixtures imported from Philadelphia were originally designed for gas and later converted for electricity. There was a two-story stone carriage house in the rear. The lot extended to the San Antonio River. The San Antonio *Express* in describing the house said, "Major Kampmann has taken especial pains in the construction of this building and it is indeed a monument to his skill."[41] Kampmann's daughter Eda wrote in her diary of touring the newly completed mansion and seeing the elegant interior with "the very best and most expensive carpets, furniture, fire places, etc. [. . .] The interior alone cost twenty-five thousand dollars."[42]

Carl and Hulda Moureau Groos raised nine children in this house. He was president of the Groos Bank from 1874, and along with his brothers, a prominent member of the Casino Club. Carl died in 1892, and Groos heirs lived in the house until 1948. It was then purchased by the San Antonio Area Girl Scouts and served as the Girl Scouts headquarters in

Bexar County, called "Martha Manor," from 1957 to 1981. Charles Butt then purchased it and carefully restored and remodeled the house and landscaping with Ford Powell Carson. The house is part of the King William Historic District, listed on the National Register of Historic Places, and a designated Texas Historic Landmark.

Victorian Commercial Buildings

During the two decades after the Civil War, Kampmann also built a small number of Victorian commercial buildings for clients including William Bennett (1870), Francois Guilbeau, August Staacke (1874), and Baetz & Lange (1876) on or near Commerce Street in San Antonio. These were warehouses, salesrooms, and administrative offices for small local companies. Staacke sold carriages and farm equipment, while Baetz & Lange was a carriage shop run by two blacksmiths/wheelwrights who commissioned Kampmann to build a stone building to replace their original shop behind the Alamo after it burned down.[43] Very little is left of the original Kampmann buildings, as the businesses were very much tied to the technology and needs of the day. When that technology changed, the business evolved and outgrew their facilities or disappeared.[44]

In 1879, Kampmann worked with architect Alfred Giles on the Faltin Store in Comfort in Kendall County, Texas, for fellow German immigrant Friedrich August Faltin. Faltin and Schreiner established a successful mercantile business in 1869. The enterprise grew to be a successful company in Texas. The little general store that included a bank and post office became a landmark in that small town. The building has survived both fires and changing business trends due to the nature of the tourist town economy, good management as a family business in a small town, as well as a strong preservation ethic and Giles's reputation. It was restored by August Faltin III and is a Recorded Texas Historic Landmark.

The building was a Victorian Italian gem of local limestone, built when Faltin bought out Schreiner's interest in the partnership in Comfort in

1879. The two-story building included a full-basement warehouse (with a freight elevator), the general store on the first floor, and a home for the Faltin family on the second floor above the shop. Tall shuttered, double-hung windows that could serve as doors opened onto the porch and balcony, providing access as well as ventilation and giving the façade a distinctive German Hill Country appearance. The first-floor windows

Fig 81. Faltin Store, Comfort, with Alfred Giles, 1879 [author]

were capped with Italianate hooded segmental arches. Alfred Giles chose thin piers with decorative millwork on the porch and balcony, and an arched cornice. Giles also designed the addition in 1907, which extended the façade and repeated the same motifs.

These buildings re-established Kampmann's reputation as a pre-eminent builder and a leading businessman in San Antonio. He would capitalize on this reputation while building his standing in the community over the next years.

REFLECTED
CEILING.

CHAMBER

CHAMBER

12'-0"

DOWN
19 R.

12'-0"

Reflected Cl'g.

2"x8" 3'-6" O.C.

18'-0"

13'-3½"

3'-6"

13'-3½"

1'-6"

17'-11"

1'-1"

1'-6"

1"x6" Cypress D.&M.floor

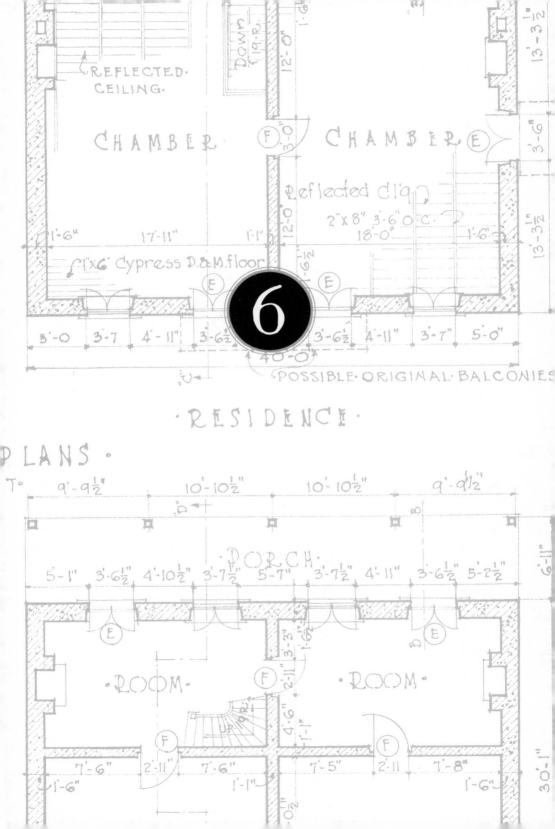

E

E

6½"

3'-0"

F

E

3'-0"

E

3'-6½"

5'-0"

3'-7"

4'-11"

3'-6½"

3'-6½"

4'-11"

3'-7"

5'-0"

40'-0"

POSSIBLE ORIGINAL BALCONIES

· R E S I D E N C E ·

· P L A N S ·

9'-9½"

10'-10½"

10'-10½"

9'-9½"

6'-11"

5'-1"

3'-6½"

4'-10½"

3'-7½"

· P O R C H ·

5'-7"

3'-7½"

4'-11"

3'-6½"

5'-2½"

E

E

3'-3"

· R O O M ·

F

UP 21 R

· R O O M ·

6½"

F

4'-6"

1'-1"

F

7'-6"

2'-11"

7'-6"

7'-5"

2'-11"

7'-8"

1'-6"

1'-1"

1'-6"

30'-1"

Entrepreneur and
Public Persona
1870–1885

———— ◄)•●•(► ————

John Kampmann was an imposing figure in many ways. Physically, he was six feet tall and weighed 225 pounds.[1] Publically, he was prominent and wealthy, connected in one way or another to virtually every civic, economic, and social circle in the city. The last phase of his life was spent in semiretirement from building, contracting, and supplying materials to other builders. He had always been involved in the construction of public buildings and establishing a presence in the community, but during his last two decades especially, he focused on new business opportunities from the management perspective, as well as civic commissions and involvement in municipal politics. These interests overlapped.

He also had a substantial portfolio to oversee. By 1877, "the Major ranked as the third largest real estate owner in San Antonio—trailing only the Maverick Estate and the firm of Adams and Wicks—with properties assessed at $198,000 [equivalent to over $4 million today]."[2] This was before he acquired ownership of the Menger Hotel in 1881, as well as returns on corporate investments. He had long been acquiring prime real estate throughout the city and in neighboring areas, which became increasingly valuable. He continued buying, selling, and swapping land, including gifts to family members, until his death, at which time his estate was estimated to be worth $1 million (equivalent to over $23 million today).[3]

Public Service

Kampmann's first involvement with local politics was in the 1850s when he joined the "Bombshell Democrats" in opposition to Mayor (and recent client) James R. Sweet and his administration. Sweet was elected on a slate put up by the Native American Party, or "Know Nothings" as they were referred to. This party was infamous for opposing foreigners, immigrants, and Catholics, which did nothing for their reputation among the German community. But Kampmann declined to endorse the Bombshell's candidate, J. M. Devine, and instead joined former mayor John Carolan's "People's Ticket," running for a seat on the city council himself. Carolan lost by fifty-four votes.

A decade later, local politics were dominated by the veil of Reconstruction policies. The Republican military governor replaced the Democratic mayor and city council with his appointees, including William C. A. Thielepape as mayor. While the Reconstruction Republicans' agenda was to promote economic development, San Antonians, especially Germans, were divided between resentment over how they came to power and agreement with their program. Kampmann's interests were pro-business (especially his) no matter which side was promoting it.

In 1870, James P. Newcomb, former San Antonio alderman and newly appointed Texas secretary of state, wrote a new city charter for his hometown that increased local governmental power. Businessmen, including Kampmann, were opposed to it and formed a coalition to fight back in the press and in public meetings, resulting in a new alliance. The 1870 municipal election resulted in the selection of an African-American, former Kampmann employee and Republican-endorsed J. W. Mozee, who was named as alderman from the Third Ward. But, after much controversy, the governor replaced Mozee and the entire city council in March, 1872. Kampmann was then appointed as alderman to the Third Ward and served two terms.

Although he retired from elected public service after those two terms, Kampmann continued to appear in the public arena and before city council, as well as in court, on more personal matters, sometimes bringing petitions and other times responding to summonses. With Ed Steves he advocated paving streets, and he urged the city to work on bringing the railroad to San Antonio and to inaugurate a streetcar system. He was one of the parties accused of "defiling the waters of the Alamo Ditch" in 1883; charges were dropped in return for his promise to keep the area clean in the future.[4] He offered to "put up a fine fountain as a donation to the city" in Alamo Plaza, provided the city would remove "the old unsightly market stall at the center."[5] He consistently encouraged endorsement of proposals for new development downtown, especially along Commerce, on which he owned much property. He also accepted public service assignments, including serving on a state-appointed committee in 1883 to inspect the new Texas Capitol (which the committee found failing on a number of counts).[6]

Civic Commissions and Civic Affairs
1860 Commerce Street Bridge

The first of Kampmann's civic commissions was in 1860 for the Commerce Street Bridge.[7] The bridge site on Commerce Street has remained consistent, but the bridges have flooded or become outdated and been replaced several times. When the city council authorized proposals in March for a new bridge, Kampmann as contractor and Fries as architect submitted a joint proposal and won the contract. The deadline for completion of the bridge was February 1861, which was met.[8]

The handsome new bridge was made of iron—the first in San Antonio. Kampmann was concerned about the grading done by the subcontractor and petitioned the city to relieve him of any liability due to drainage problems, to which they agreed. In fact, there were drainage problems, and the city again contracted Kampmann to finish the bridge and construct sidewalks in 1868. Kampmann had a history of troubles

Fig 82. The cast iron bridge on Commerce Street separated pedestrians from wheeled vehicles, ca. 1907. [95-502 UTSA SC]

surrounding that bridge, beginning with nonpayment for services. Fries and Kampmann had to petition the city for payment. According to the tax rolls, Kampmann was not charged property taxes in 1865, which may have been part of the city's payment plan. Kampmann also received many tickets for speeding, "driving furiously" and recklessly across the bridge.[9] In response to an 1867 citation, Kampmann threatened to sue the city for not paying him the full amount owed to him on the bridge. O. Henry used the "little iron bridge" as the setting for his short story, "A Fog in Santone," published in *Cosmopolitan* in October 1912, and it came to be known as "O. Henry's Bridge." In 1914, the bridge was replaced with a concrete bridge to make way for the widening of Commerce St., and the original iron truss bridge was relocated to Johnson Street in King William, where it still carries pedestrians across the river.

Fig 83. The Commerce Street Bridge was removed to Johnson Street in King William, where it was altered, but still serves as a footbridge across the river [Bruce Harms, Historic American American Engineering Record (HAER 102-2), 2001]

1869–73 Rincon School
for Colored Children

701 N. Rincon [St Mary's] St./Convent [demolished]

Kampmann constructed the first free public school for African American children in San Antonio; he was awarded the contract, perhaps, because of his alliance with the Reconstruction Republicans. The school was open to African American students of all ages who were denied admission to the other four public schools in the city. The two-story soft rock building, described in the San Antonio *Herald* as an "elegant building," was built on the river near the Ursuline Convent.[10] The school had four teachers and four classrooms with a capacity for two hundred students, but was often overcrowded by half.[11] The initial building cost of $12,000 was financed by the Freedmen's Bureau, a federal agency initiated by President Abraham Lincoln and established by the US Congress to assist former slaves in acquiring housing, employment, and education. According to San Antonio Independent School District (SAISD) records, $4,000 came "from the proceeds of the sale of an abandoned Confederate tannery."[12]

The school came under city administration in 1871. Secondary education was introduced in 1899, thanks to a monetary donation by George Breckenridge. In 1890, the name was changed to Riverside Negro School,

Fig 84. Rincon School, the first free public school for African American children, is marked #15. Kampmann's Planing Mill (#33) is across the acequia from his house. Kampmann built several other houses in this neighborhood. [Koch 1873]. There is a historic plaque marking the spot where the building stood. The school moved to a new site in 1914 and was renamed the Douglass Academy. [Koch, 1873]

and then in 1904 to Frederick Douglass School in honor of the abolitionist, civil rights worker, and social reformer. The school was relocated in 1914 to a new building at what is now 318 Martin Luther King Drive on the East Side. The original building was sold to help pay for the new school and then torn down.[13]

1872–78 Alamo Literary Society
Corner of Jefferson and Houston Streets

Organized in 1869 and incorporated two years later, the Alamo Literary and Scientific Society was San Antonio's first learned society, organized chiefly by Samuel Maverick and chemist George Kalteyer.[14] In 1873, the two disciplines split and the San Antonio Literary Society became a separate entity. The Samuel Maverick Estate had donated a lot at the northwest corner of Jefferson and Houston Streets to the society on which they could erect a building. Dr. George Cupples described this legacy in his eulogy of Maverick given to the society in 1870:

> To this Society he leaves the signal honor of having inscribed his name on the roll of its founders, and the task of rearing on the site, which you owe to his munificence, an edifice which may do honor to the donor and credit to your young Association, the Alamo Literary Society; a task in which I trust you will be aided by the wealthier members of the community.[15]

A letter from Sidney Lanier to his father in 1872 described the association as "a flourishing institution [. . .] which is now building a hall to cost some $13,000, and of which I have become an active member."[16] For a one dollar fee and twenty-five cents a month, subscribers could borrow books and use the hall and reading rooms for discussion of intellectual ideas or current events. The library also provided public access to their collection. It was open from 4:00 to 6:00 p.m. Mondays and Thursdays for women, and 8:00 to 10:00 p.m. Tuesdays and Fridays for men. Vinton L. James remembered it as, "the first real estate development on Houston Street [. . .] an ugly soft rock one-story building, which enclosed a large room with a stage that was used for theatrical performances, and the floor for dancing parties and political gatherings."[17] In 1878, it was the site of the first appearance in San Antonio of Thomas Edison's phonograph. The hall was more successful as a theatrical venue than a literary society and became the impetus for the construction of the Opera House on Alamo Plaza in 1886.

Meanwhile, the society itself was floundering. While seventy-five hundred volumes had been assembled, frequent statements in the newspapers in the 1880s urged the establishment of a true public library, complaining that the Literary Society library was never available because of the absence of the librarian, while members criticized that "several thousand volumes [were] unavailable—locked up in Col. Williams's residence."[18]

According to Vinton James, Kampmann's "building was never finished according to the plans, and Mr. Kampmann, to get his money expended for the ugly building, became the owner for a song on account of non-payment."[19] The society had to mortgage the property for $9,000 to finance construction. Kampmann held a builder's lien, and the society lost its property to the lien holder.[20] The society relocated to 45 Commerce Street, where they operated a lending library administered by John H. Copeland, but "its career soon ended for want of financial support."[21]

Kampmann let the San Antonio Dramatic Hall use the building for a while. He had plans for converting the building into an opera house, but they never materialized. Instead, it was used as a grocery and Aiken's fruit store, where there was a fire in 1886. The remains of the building were torn down in 1890 and replaced with four large stores and the Jefferson Hotel, owned by the Kampmann Estate.[22]

1872 Fire Company #2
115 Avenue C [Broadway]

Until 1891, when a paid firefighting force was established, San Antonio relied on civic-minded individuals and property owners to fight fires.

Volunteers were not paid, although city council reimbursed individual expenses, and citizens often donated buckets, pumpers, and ladders. The first volunteer fire department, called the Ben Milam Company, was organized in 1854. In 1858, they acquired a hand-operated fire engine to supplant the bucket brigade. Following a disastrous fire at Eckenroth's store the next year, the Turnverein met and pledged $2,000 to establish an East Side Hose Company, renamed Alamo Fire Association No. 2, to fight fires on the east side of the river.[23] Membership was composed of German volunteers (including Kampmann friends and clients Menger, Stumberg, Degen, Steves, and Zuschlag), whose houses, businesses, and clubs were centered downtown near the Alamo. William Menger and H. D. Stumberg wrote the constitution and by-laws for the new company, temporarily housed in a shed owned by Menger at the corner of Elm and St. Joseph's.

Assistant Chief William Menger purchased a $4,000 steam pumper and (Honorary) Chief John H. Kampmann bought a Silsby Rotary steam fire engine, which was named in honor of Mayor James H. French.[24] In 1872, Kampmann built a new two-story fire station for Company No. 2 on Avenue C [Broadway] between Houston and Travis with arched doors for the fire trucks (see fig. 85). Horses were not kept on site. Instead, the firefighters commandeered the nearest team as needed to pull the fire engine to the site where volunteers showed up in nightclothes, work clothes, or party clothes, depending on the hour they were summoned.[25] Until 1878, they drew water from the river or the nearest ditch and pumped it to the site of the fire. If that site was farther away than the length of the hose, water was relayed in buckets. Thereafter, the waterworks supplied hydrants.

The Turnverein organized a hook and ladder team capable of fighting a two-story fire in 1869 and volunteered their services, since they were all athletes. Facilities were housed directly behind the main building, and a watchtower was added later. Station No. 2 hosted annual celebrations, including Washington's Birthday and Fourth of July, and also participated in every other excuse for a parade. By 1935, the station had been relocated, and the remodeled building housed the Commonwealth Bank and Trust, although it still contained the original walls.[26]

Fig 85. Firemen with equipment in front of Firehouse Company No. 2 on Avenue C, ca. 1880s. [F.A. Schmidt, 86-512 UTSA SC]

By the 1880s, there were four volunteer fire companies—two white and two African American (Companies No. 3 and No. 4). In 1878, Company No. 3 elected Kampmann as their fire chief to represent their interests before city council.[27] Council refused to cover the black units' expenses but still decided they were too heavy a burden on municipal resources, and the company was disbanded in 1888.

Eventually there were six volunteer companies, each assigned to a different part of town. When the fire bell rang out, the number of peals indicated which ward the fire was in and summoned fire companies and spectators alike. In 1891, the city switched to a professional (paid) fire department. The story of volunteer firefighting in San Antonio, unlike many other cities, was fairly clean and said more about the "conservative political and economic interests" and rivalries of its membership than gang rivalry and illegal acts, including arson, such as that found in other cities.[28]

1875 County Poor House Rock Quarry Road

[2316 Jones Avenue]

Kampmann spent the summer of 1875 working on the County Poor House near the northern city limits. The Texas State Constitution of 1869 required that each county provide a Manual Labor Poorhouse for the poor and indigent.[29] As in most Western states, Texas found it more cost effective to build a publically owned house supervised by a public employee (often a jailer) than to subsidize private citizens for providing room and board to those who fell on hard times. Counties in Texas tended to build work farms instead of single houses, as was the model in Eastern cities. The 1885 and 1914 San Antonio City Directories list the poorhouse on the west side of Rock Quarry Road, and Augustus Koch identified the four simple buildings that comprised the facility in his 1886 map.

Typical poorhouses would contain rooms (often referred to as cells); dining facilities; a kitchen; a garden; a "pesthouse" for isolating communicable diseases, especially smallpox; and a cemetery.[30] Most poorhouses died out during the Depression, due to its severity and longevity. The increasing rate of unemployment accompanied by bank closures and foreclosures gave a new, broader definition to the "deserving poor." Temporary poverty became more respectable, and sympathetic federal laws and state programs provided direct relief to those in need—which was almost everyone. The San Antonio Poor House was moved farther out of town and into the county when Rock Quarry Road became increasingly valuable.[31]

New Business

Just as Kampmann had shifted from labor to management, he moved from contractor to client in his last decade. Because of his business prestige, he was invited to serve on multiple companies' boards of directors, such as the newly established San Antonio branch of the Southern Life Insurance Co. of Memphis. He also served on the boards and as president of new companies he helped establish. They needed investments, and he was a wealthy and active citizen. They often needed buildings—and he owned land.

Utilities in the last half of nineteenth-century San Antonio were organized and operated as private enterprises rather than municipal services, following the precedent set by James Sweet owning the headwaters of the San Antonio River. Kampmann's investments in these capitalist ventures acting as municipal monopolies, including the Gas Company and the Water Works, provided the basis for much of his wealth.[32] He saw these opportunities, as he did the establishment of railroad service, as a means of securing personal financial security and acting as a "booster" for the city while helping to provide fellow citizens with what they needed to live comfortably—for those who could afford it.

In January 1860, the San Antonio Gas Company was organized by "leading citizens," including (future Mayor) John French, James Vance, George Howard, John Kampmann, Francis Guilbeau, William Menger, and August Nette, most of whom were in Kampmann's circle. Kampmann served on the board of directors and as president of this profitable business from its founding until his death twenty-five years later.[33] The city ordinance authorizing construction and the use of public streets for laying pipes established the private franchise for fifty years and fixed a maximum price, to be adjusted (mostly reduced), in the future.[34] In the 1880s, the company was awarded the exclusive right to provide electricity as well; they also supplied coal and coke and sold appliances and light fixtures. Their offices were located in the Kampmann Building.

Prior to 1878 when the first water pipes were laid in the city, San Antonians depended chiefly on wells and the old irrigation ditches for water in their residences and businesses.[35] The *acéquia* ditches were reserved for drinking water and feeding crops and were not to be used for bathing or washing clothes, enforced by the City Manager of Ditches.[36] Periodic outbreaks of cholera led to repeated attempts by George Maverick, H. B. Adams, and others to improve and manage the delivery of drinking water. Finally, in July 1877, the city signed a contract with Jean Baptiste LaCoste for construction of a waterworks system using San Antonio River water, guaranteeing him a twenty-five-year franchise, which could be bought out by the city or renewed in five-year increments.[37]

Startup was expensive and customers slow to enroll. In 1879, LaCoste issued preferred stock to a few investors, who formed a board of directors, including Kampmann, Jacob Waelder, George Brackenridge, and others. LaCoste continued to rack up debts, payable to San Antonio National Bank (owned by Brackenridge and forerunner of the Lockwood and Kampmann Bank), until 1883, when he sold his interests to his banker. Brackenridge was named chairman of the new Water Works Company and had the financial capabilities to make the company successful. He owned the water rights at the head of the river and added them to the company's holdings. He aggressively dug new wells and enlarged the plant. When he deeded the land for Brackenridge and Mahncke Parks to the city, he reserved the water rights for the company. All of this coincided with improvements in indoor plumbing and the development of steam turbines, aiding demand while lowering the cost of supply. Although Brackenridge disposed of his interests in the San Antonio Water Supply Company in 1906, the city did not acquire ownership until 1925, making the investors and their heirs very wealthy for a very long time.

Kampmann was also active in securing both a railroad and streetcar system in the city, personally guaranteeing subscriptions, serving on commissions, and trying to convince the business community to support their efforts. In 1874, Kampmann and his partners received a state charter for the Bexar Street Railway Company, and the trolleys began rolling on July 4, 1878. Seven directors were elected by the stockholders, including Kampmann, Joseph Lockwood, Charles Merritt, and Jacob Waelder, and the city issued twenty-year bonds to build the infrastructure.[38]

1883 Lone Star Brewery Company
200 W. Grand [Jones] Avenue

Beer production in Texas changed drastically in the 1880s when a modern plant using new techniques forced many small beer operations out of business. At a meeting held at Fire Station No. 2 on August 6, 1883, Kampmann and five of his peers raised between $75,000 and $85,000 of the projected cost of $100,000 to launch a new brewery.[39] Kampmann, as principal stockholder, then joined with longtime friend Edward Hoppe and Adolphus Busch of St. Louis to form a stock company establishing the Lone Star Brewery on the banks of the San Antonio River. Kampmann served as president of the corporation and Hoppe served as manager. Busch introduced new technology, and together the team built the first large, mechanized brewery in the state.[40] The building, which held its grand opening on September 12, 1884, cost $150,000 and was equipped with state-of-the-art equipment, which was periodically updated.[41] It contained an ice plant, cooper shops, bathhouse, hops house, and stable, as well as brewing equipment and a warehouse. The new firm had their own bottling plant just east of the main building and a circuit through Texas and Mexico all the way to California. Degen's Brewery, on the other hand, was a one-man operation using hand-operated equipment, serving cold beer only on his own grounds within hours of production, and never exporting. Statewide production numbers skyrocketed with the new system.

Lone Star Brewery quickly became a social institution in the community. Two thousand people showed up at the grand opening on September 17, 1884, "liberally tasting the beer and partaking of the elegant banquet which was spread in the grove adjoining the brewery towards the river." Kampmann acted as a master of ceremonies, and US Marshal Harrington Lee Gosling was the "orator of the day." The Eighth Cavalry band provided the music.[42] The employees organized a society known as the Sons of Gambrinus and led at least one parade along Houston, Soledad, Commerce, and Alamo Streets. Following behind the Fashion Theatre band, Gambrinus, the unofficial patron saint of beer and brewing, led the parade astride a mammoth cask of beer, holding a foaming beaker of the malt fluid. He was surrounded by his court, representing the various ingredients and methods used in the process of brewing the great beverage. This car was followed by the corps of employees of the Lone Star brewery, eighty-seven strong. [. . .] The procession, which was a very commendable one, attracted a great deal of admiration, along its route.[43]

The architect of the original Lone Star buildings is unknown, and the original building is all but invisible now.[44] The Koch Bird's Eye Map of 1886 shows a small complex of frame buildings, most of which were replaced in 1900. The main four-story building was surrounded by support facilities and outbuildings. When new, the brewery produced three hunded barrels a day under a variety of labels.[45]

Hermann Kampmann started as treasurer in 1884 and became president following his father's death. In 1892, Adolphus A. Busch purchased the entire company.[46] The campus was enlarged in 1900 when,

Fig 86 Lone Star Brewery [Morrison, ca 1890]

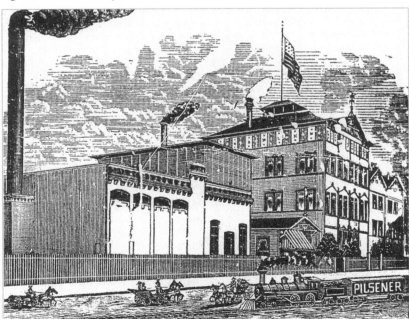

according to the San Antonio *Gazette*, many of the original wooden buildings were torn down and replaced or remodeled with pressed brick construction.[47] The commission went to E. Jungenfeld and Co. of St. Louis (Anheuser-Busch company architects), working with the San Antonio firm of Wahrenberger and Beckmann. It appears that the same rhythm of buildings sizes was maintained between the old and new construction.

The brewery was producing as many as sixty-five thousand barrels annually under a variety of labels.[48] But limitations imposed by World War I and Prohibition forced the brewery to adapt and reorganize, and the brewery never fully recovered.[49] Initially they tried introducing Tango, a soft drink to make "the palate dance with joy," but it would never replace beer.[50] The Lone Star Cotton Mill was housed in the old bottling house from 1921 to 1925, replaced by Lone Star Ice and Food. The brewery sat empty for many years but was acquired in the 1970s for use by the San Antonio Museum of Art, which opened in 1981. Cambridge Seven Associates of Massachusetts oversaw the adaptive construction, and it is once again one of the highlights of the city—this time for the display of history, art, and the river.

1882 Lockwood and Kampmann Bank

Banking in Texas was a private enterprise with very little state or federal regulation. Institutions such as Groos National Bank, D. & A. Oppenheimer, and T. C. Frost added banking as a service offered at their mercantile establishments. This arose out of the frontier lifestyle in which clients were involved with trade in Mexico and Indian Territory. Mostly this consisted of providing credit, safe deposit boxes, and currency exchange. The bank eventually became the primary focus of the business and usually stayed within the families of the founders through several generations. Kampmann entered the banking business by investing with friends and associates.

W. A. Bennett, for whom Kampmann built a three-story office building, had been a prosperous steamboat owner in Missouri when he moved to San Antonio and established the first bank in the city in 1865: the W. A. Bennett Bank. J. T. Thornton, a banker from Independence, Missouri, joined him and formed Bennett & Thornton. Joseph S. Lockwood, a banker from New York, organized the San Antonio National Bank with George Brackenridge in 1866. Lockwood then organized a private bank, which was eventually consolidated with the previous bank as Bennett, Thornton, and Lockwood. When Bennett died, Thornton moved to Kansas City, and Lockwood acquired sole proprietorship as Lockwood National Bank. He soon joined with John Kampmann and formed Lockwood & Kampmann (see fig. 87–88).[51]

When Kampmann joined the firm, the bank was located at the corner of Commerce and Yturri Streets. They boasted an imposing yet comfortable banking room with a fireplace. A large set of scales weighed bullion and silver, and each teller had a six-shooter in his drawer, in addition to access to a double-barrel shotgun behind the rail. They also possessed one of the

Fig 87. Ad for Lockwood & Kampmann Bank [San Antonio City Directory]

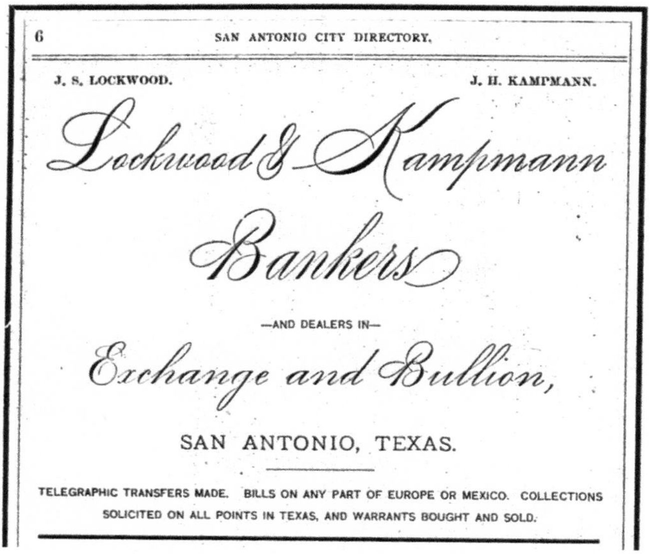

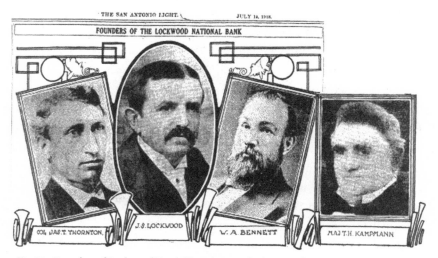

Fig 88. Founders of Lockwood Bank [San Antonio Light, 1918]

few burglarproof safes in the city, shipped from New York to Indianola, then hauled by oxen to San Antonio. Bennett, Thornton, and Lockwood had installed a smooth cement walkway in front of the bank in contrast to the flagstone sidewalks along Commerce. Bennett's son Max set a silver dollar in the wet cement in front of the front door for good luck.

When Kampmann added his name to the bank, they agreed a more modern image was needed, and the new partner set about arranging for a new building to be the centerpiece of San Antonio business activity.

Fig 89 Blank check from Lockwood Bank, ca 1880 [courtesy of Judith Carrington]

The location was at the corner of Commerce and Soledad Streets across from Main Plaza and the San Fernando Cathedral, on the site of the old Haas & Oppenheimer Dry Goods. This was the Kampmann Building, or Kampmann Block as it was called when it was built; the bank occupied the building until 1891.[52]

1883–84 Kampmann Block
Corner of West Commerce and Soledad Streets

Kampmann's last tangible contribution to San Antonio during his lifetime was considered the city's first skyscraper: the Kampmann Block, built to showcase the Lockwood & Kampmann Bank.[53] He designed the building and worked as contractor while also providing the cream-colored limestone from the Geronimo Creek Quarry he owned near Helotes. The San Antonio *Light* proclaimed the recently completed fireproof building the "finest, most costly and complete in the State of Texas, and worthy of a place beside the grand structures of the great Northern and Eastern cities."[54]

The four-story building (plus basement) opened in December 1884. It was the most modern building in town, "evidence of how progressive San Antonio" was, setting the standard for all that came after it.[55] The local newspapers described it as "one of the finest ornaments of this city."[56]

The ground floor was faced with thirty-inch thick, rough-cut stone with arched openings, like an Italian palazzo banking house, and the remaining three floors dressed with smooth cut stone. Windows on the upper floors featured carved stone surrounds with Renaissance caps of three different shapes, one for each floor. The corner of the building was chamfered so the entry faced the plaza. New buildings on the other two corners later followed suit. The decorated cornice was topped by a pediment with the simple announcement of "BANK."

Lockwood and Kampmann Bank occupied the entire ninety-nine-foot ground floor along Soledad, as well as the basement. The

*Fig 90.
Kampmann
Building under
construction
[courtesy of Judith
Carrington]*

*Fig 91.
Kampmann
Building, ca. 1900
[San Antonio
Light Collection
L-1228-G UTSA
SC]*

Fig 92. Kampmann Building kitty corner from Main Plaza [Library of Congress, 1890]

one-hundred-foot frontage on Commerce hosted the Galveston, Harrisburg, and San Antonio Railway Company, and Bell & Brothers Jewelry. Fifty-one offices inside were all supplied with gas, water, and steam heating. The building contained the first passenger elevator in the city, patented by Otis and installed by Hall & Co. of Chicago.[57] The tellers' windows in the bank were of decorated brass, and the floors were mosaic tiles. The bank office also contained two large safes, both "fitted with time locks of the most approved and latest patterns, and are both burglar and fire proof."[58] A third safe located in the basement, also with a time lock, served as the safety deposit vault. The vault had a steel lining protecting four hundred safety deposit boxes, of which it was said, "the most skillful and determined burglar would find an attempt to break it open fruitless."[59] The massive front doors of the building were made of steel, and each contained a series of six locks that could be unfastened with a single movement.[60]

The building soon became the most prestigious address for new companies, professional offices, and law firms, as Kampmann had predicted. Its presence attracted new restaurants, drugstores, cigar shops, and billiard parlors to the vicinity. Situated between the old county courthouse on Soledad Street and the Federal Court in the French Building, it was a convenient and popular arrangement for law offices and the site of politicians "lining up their forces for the next campaign."[61]

City offices were also housed there beginning in 1885, and city council met on the fourth floor until the new city hall was completed in 1891. When the Fourth Court of Civic Appeals was established in 1893, they met on the fourth floor of the Kampmann Building every Wednesday morning until the new courthouse was completed across Main Plaza in 1896.[62] Forty-two years later, Fred Mosebach recalled covering their first session on September 5, 1893. "The old building still stands in its original form as constructed more than 50 years ago, and is the [first and] last of San Antonio's skyscrapers of those days."[63]

Lockwood [and Kampmann] Bank was replaced by Alamo National Bank and later the National Bank of Commerce, which occupied the site until 1918. The top two floors were removed ca. 1940 when the H & I Improvement Company took on a ten-year lease to convert the building into a modern department store trimmed in black Carrara and aluminum and requiring large display windows on the first floor, as well as additional entrances. Over the years the building lost more and more of its integrity and beauty. Signage forced the removal of more details, and the façade was plastered over completely. It is almost unrecognizable today.

The partial shell that occupies the location today is a far cry from the original as described in a contemporary newspaper account written at the opening of the Kampmann Building in December 1884:

> The only fault connected with it is that owing to the narrow street the beautiful façades do not come to that prominence which they so richly deserve. Nevertheless Mr. Kampmann has built himself a monument that will remind future generations of its projector and builder, and also recall to them the first and most successful contractor and builder of San Antonio.[64]

Fig 93 (above). Kampmann Building being decapitated, 1940 [L-2291-F UTSA SC]
Fig 94 (below). Top floor demolition, 1940 [L-2291-G UTSA SC]

Fig 95. Kampmann Building gutted, 1940s [Estate of Robert Moss Ayres, 83-467 UTSA SC]

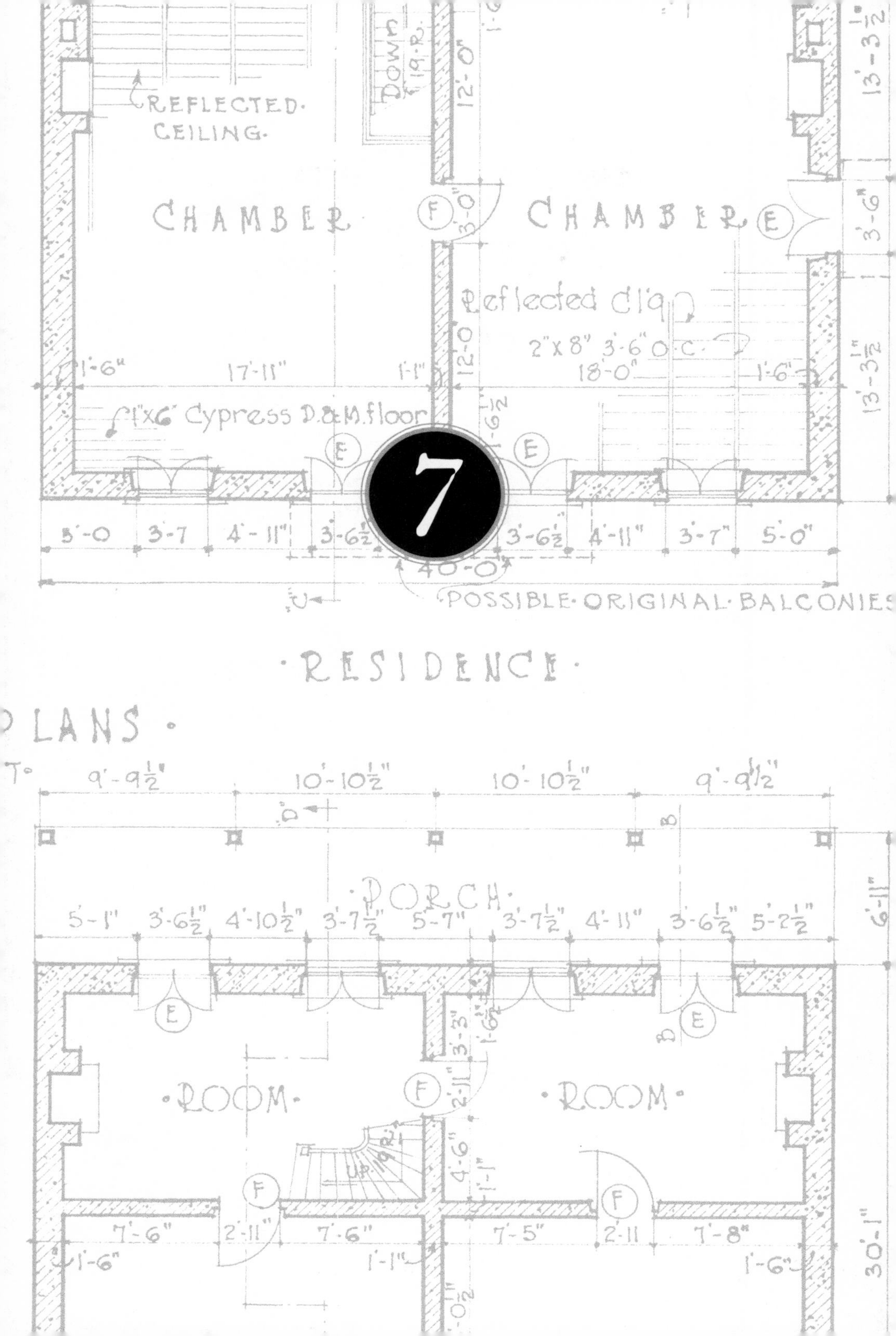

CRELFECTED.
CEILING.

CHAMBER. $\quad$ F $\quad$ CHAMBER E

3'-0"

Reflected cl'ag

2"x8" 3'-6" O.C.

1'-6" 17'-11" 1'-1" 18'-0" 1'-6"

13'-3½"

3'-6"

12'-0"

13'-3½"

6½"

f 1"x6" Cypress D.&M. floor

E $\quad$ **7** $\quad$ E

5'-0 3'-7 4'-11" 3'-6½" 40'-0" 3'-6½" 4'-11" 3'-7" 5'-0"

POSSIBLE ORIGINAL BALCONIES

· R E S I D E N C E ·

P L A N S .

9'-9½" 10'-10½" 10'-10½" 9'-9½"

· P O R C H ·

6'-11"

5'-1" 3'-6½" 4'-10½" 3'-7½" 5'-7" 3'-7½" 4'-11" 3'-6½" 5'-2½"

E $\quad$ E

·ROOM· F ·ROOM·

3'-3"

F UP 10 R. F

4'-6"

30'-1"

7'-6" 2'-11" 7'-6" 7'-5" 2'-11 7'-8"

1'-6" 1'-1" 1'-6"

Legacy

———)·•·(———

In the latter years of his life, John Kampmann retired and devoted time to raising high-grade Jersey cattle. He bought a tract of land close to town, where he erected a summer home, and where he seemed to delight in spending quiet days attending to his stock.[1] The ranch was on Salado Creek, just east of the city. When it later became the site of the Woodland Golf Club in 1924, his grandson Robert S. Kampmann, San Antonio's leading amateur golfer, drove the first ball at the new course.[2]

John Kampmann died rather unexpectedly on September 6, 1885, while on vacation in Colorado Springs, ironically on a trip to aid his wife's health. He was eulogized as "a useful and worthy citizen, whose place it will be hard to fill," and his death was described as "a loss [San Antonio] can ill afford and one not to be forgotten for many long years."[3]

Pallbearers included military officers, aldermen, senators, friends, and clients, and the music was provided by the 8th Cavalry Band. The mile-and-a-quarter-long cortege was led by Fire Chief Duerler and Asst. Chief H. L. Duerler, then more firemen, members of Masonic lodges, Rt. Rev. Bishop Elliott, and Dean Richardson, both of the Episcopal church. The hearse, drawn by four black horses, was followed by scores of carriages,

Fig 96. John H. Kampmann [Robert Onderdonk, courtesy of Don and Lou Celia Frost]

Fig 97. Caroline Kampmann [E. Raba, courtesy of Judith Carrington]

*Fig 98. Kampmann Family Plot, Masonic Cemetery, San Antonio. The symbol atop the
headstone appears to be that of the Ancient Order of United Workmen (AOUW), a Masonic
mutual protection society established in 1868, which joined employers and employees in the
protection of the working class. [author]*

buggies, and citizens on foot. Many businesses closed their doors out of respect, and the procession was lined with thousands of mourners. The Episcopalian funeral rites, led by Elliott and Richardson, were accompanied by
the Masonic burial service and funerary anthems sung by the Beethoven
Männerchor. He was buried with other members of his family in the Masonic Cemetery, the spot later marked by a granite marker.[4]

Caroline Bonnet Kampmann lived until 1914 and continued to
manage the Kampmann properties, buying, selling, and developing.
She was also active in social and charitable events, working especially
hard with her daughter-in-law Lizzie to raise money for the Protestant
Home for Destitute Children, of which Lizzie was director. Caroline was

an ardent suffragist, and dozens of her heirs honored her memory by naming their daughters after her. When she died in 1914, there was a full-page obituary in the San Antonio newspaper, which estimated her estate to be worth $1 million (the equivalent of $23 million today).[5] Much of the Kampmanns' property was sold at great profit for later developments on the edges of the city, such as Laurel Heights, Jefferson Heights, Eastland Heights, and Alamo Heights. There are still a handful of Kampmann Street, Boulevard, and Avenue signs in parts of the city where they owned land.

Daughter Eda Kampmann married Dr. John Herff in 1875. He died seven years later, and Eda went on to marry Theodore Meyer of St. Louis. John and Eda's surviving son, John Bennett Herff, also became a prominent doctor. He married Florence Harris from St. Louis and they had three children: Carolyn, who married August Herff, Jr.; Florence Ilse, who married Thomas Clayborne Frost; and Jean, who married James Henderson.[6] The Herff descendants are still very active in Boerne, where they have preserved the Herff Ranch and established the Cibolo Nature Center.

Son Hermann Kampmann inherited his father's business sense, much of his property, and several of his business interests.[7] In addition to serving on multiple boards of directors for San Antonio companies founded by his father, as well as many other new businesses, he was a partner in the Lockwood-Kampmann Bank and owner of both San Antonio Gas and San Antonio Electric Light Companies. He sold most of these interests to become full-time manager of the Menger Hotel until his death in 1902. He married Elizabeth "Lizzie" Simpson in 1880. She was president of the first Battle of the Flowers and active in many social clubs and charities. They had three children: Isaac (Ike) Simpson Kampmann, who married Margaret Adams; Eda Kampmann, the first Fiesta Queen of the Order of the Alamo, who married Joseph Hardin Frost; and Robert Simpson Kampmann, a local golf champion who married Marion Weaver and returned to San Antonio in his later years to manage the Menger Hotel. The Frosts continued their involvement with Frost Bank in San Antonio. Many of Ike's descendants became attorneys in San Antonio. His daughter Carolyn Adams Kampmann married Garland Lasater. The Lasaters continued operation of the Falfurrias Creamery Company dairy ranch, established by Edward C. Lasater (Carolyn Adams Kampmann's father-in-law), who also founded the city of Falfurrias and Brook County.

Son Gus Kampmann married Emilie Elmendorf. They had two sons, Arthur and Edwin Kampmann, but the marriage ended in divorce, and in 1889, Gus married Laura Campman of New Orleans. He had a temper, which was displayed in numerous public disagreements, both private arguments and political causes including anti-Prohibition. He was involved in a number of businesses in town, including managing both the Kampmann Mill and the Mackey Brick and Tile Co. of Calaveras, Texas, which maintained an office in the Menger Hotel. Both he and Hermann were investors in the tile company; Gus moved to Calaveras to supervise brick-making operations for Mackey Tile and eventually moved to Mexico.[8]

The names of John and Caroline Bonnet Kampmann's scions, including Kampmann, Herff, Frost, Chipman, Carrington, and Lasater, and family members, including Boelhauwe and Bonnet, are still well known in San Antonio, the Hill Country, throughout Texas, and on the East Coast.

John Hermann Kampmann was the right man in the right place at the right time with the necessary skills and connections, as well as the drive and ambition to use them. He was willing to work hard and to take risks when he deemed them appropriate. He was more of an entrepreneur and business booster than architect. He knew how to leverage opportunities and accomplishments to establish his own career and build a bigger city.

He also gave back to the city that had been so good to him, in the form of public service and private charity. John and Caroline donated one acre near the head of the river to the Benevolent Society of German Ladies in 1884.[9] After his death, Caroline continued to donate land and money to public causes, including land for a courthouse extension in 1891 and the new Carnegie Library built in 1903. Kampmann's contributions at the time were seen as a businessman's devotion to promoting private enterprise and building the business community, beginning with the Menger Hotel.

But it is his work as a physical builder that interests me more. As a stonemason, contractor, construction supervisor, builder, and architect, he helped change the face of the city from mostly adobe Spanish to one mixed with German limestone construction. He and other German immigrants established a strong German community and gave it a face. They kept their culture alive and successfully amalgamated it with other ethnic groups that arrived before and after them, just as they mixed the German building traditions with the Texas climate and materials and the American architectural styles.

Kampmann and other German builders gave the city a vernacular German Texan architecture, a regional expression of the Greek Revival style. The more formal version of this style was popular in America between 1820 and 1860 for a number of reasons and was the first nationally popular style not limited to one part of the country. Coming out of the War of 1812, American culture was increasingly breaking away from England and searching for a cultural reflection of independence. Greece was the birthplace of democracy. Americans identified with the Greek Revolution against Turkey, and architects appreciated the purity and order of Greek architecture, which replaced Thomas Jefferson's favored Roman Revival. Greek Revival was simple to build, recognizable by everyone, and examples and details were readily available in carpenters' handbooks.

While there was a national standard—columns supporting a pediment—the rules allowed for regional variations and interpretations of the Greek symbolism. In the Deep South, this resulted in two-storied balconies supported by giant columns in the plantation's Great House. The structure encouraged ventilation, and it looked great atop a hill or at the end of tree-lined *allée*. Yet while the Classical form said "Important Building Here," it is questionable whether slaves would have read it as a sign of freedom from tyranny or of independence and democracy.

Besides the governor's mansion and a couple of houses in Austin, all by Abner Cook, there wasn't much formal Greek Revival in Texas, especially in South Texas. What Kampmann and others did was develop the traditional European colonial house, consisting of one room on either side of a central hallway. When that central space was part of the house, as in New England and the mid-Atlantic, it was called a hall and parlor house. As families became larger and more established, a kitchen could be added to the rear, making a saltbox, and bedrooms upstairs, making it a foursquare. In hot and humid areas such as Texas and Louisiana, the central hallway might be left open at either end, creating a dogtrot house, so named because dogs (or people) could sleep in the covered but ventilated center between the hall and the parlor.

Kampmann, using thick limestone that was readily available and easy to cut, and tall windows and doors aligned with counterparts on the opposite walls, enclosed the dogtrot open space. In large houses of one or two stories, the rooms opened to the hallway, and if the front and back doors were open, one could capture a breeze. Smaller houses followed the German tradition, wherein the rooms opened outward to a connecting gallery like French settlement and Cajun houses. He then turned that gallery into a covered front porch, deep enough for rocking chairs and a swing. The porch (and later the second-story balcony) was articulated into three to five bays, with the wooden piers supporting the roof. The pediment above the columns was an optical illusion created by the main façade rising above the porch in a triangular shape or repeating the horizontal edge with a thick entablature defining the cornice. He had a good eye for proportion and scale, as seen in the Sweet, Eagar, and Kampmann Houses.

With the advent of the Industrial Revolution, circular saws and jigsaws were used to make decorated gingerbread patterns for the front face. The arrival of the railroad in San Antonio enabled the importation of standardized decoration and pre-sawn lumber for the new planing mills. Prefabricated as well as handmade ornamentations were now available at a much lower cost and were therefore applied liberally to every building. Thus, previously plain façades were given more status through delicate capitals and garlands, creating a Victorian version of the Greek Revival, as seen in the Steves and Groos Houses. The same embellishment could turn an L-shaped Plains Cottage with an inset porch into a Victorian Vernacular version of Queen Anne. This trend is clearly seen in the evolution of Kampmann's buildings over three decades.

Kampmann was a master builder or "housewright" (a common nineteenth-century term for house builder) who began referring to himself as an architect, at that time a word synonymous with builder. Architects, like builders, stonemasons, and carpenters, learned their craft while serving apprenticeships to experienced designers and builders. According to Joan Ockman, who cited *The Builder's Dictionary*, published in 1734,

> an architect was 'a Master Workman in a Building, he who designs the Model, or draws the Plot, Plan or Draught of the whole Fabrick; whose Business it is to consider the whole Manner and Method of the Building; and also to compute the Charge and Expence [sic].' An architect, that is, was a man whose business lay in making the drawings and estimates needed to construct a building and oversee the construction process.[10]

This Kampmann did frequently. Until the late nineteenth century, "architect" with a lower case "a" referred to a designer, originator, planner, or overseer; it was used to describe a construction supervisor, or one who was trained to plan and design buildings and to oversee their construction. In fact, the term originated in the sixteenth century from the Greek *arkhitektōn* (*arckhi* = chief and *tektōn* = builder). Therefore, master builders frequently referred to themselves as architects. With a capital "A," the term now refers to a licensed professional, reflecting the evolving nomenclature of the late nineteenth century.[11] Spiro Kostof defined the architect as the "conceiver of buildings," whose "primary task [historically] as now, is to communicate what proposed buildings should be and look like [. . . and whose] role is that of mediator between the client or patron [. . .] and the work force."[12]

The history of the architectural profession, especially in a democratic America, involved a long struggle for recognition and regulation through educating and licensing, resulting eventually in the establishment of the AIA and the creation of state regulation.[13] Largely, this was a matter of recognizing the designer's time, creativity, and service as worthy of financial compensation, whether the commission was completed or not, as opposed to the practice of paying the carpenter or mason for what was physically built. Craftsmanship required expertise, but was only compensated when there was a finished product. The AIA today advocates professional standards; has a voice in the accreditation of architecture schools; raises public awareness about the importance of the profession; and coordinates contracts, documentation, and state licensing within the profession. With the legal status of a professional one may not use the title "architect" unless he or she is licensed.

Kampmann and his nineteenth-century contemporaries, including François Giraud, Wilhelm C. A. Thielepape, John Fries, Gustav Friesleben, and even Alfred Giles, found themselves in an ambiguous area between the craft of carpentry and the profession of architecture. All but Giles were trained primarily as journeymen, craftsmen, and engineers. Kampmann had a professional education but saw himself as part of the building trade, preferring management to manual labor. There were no architecture schools in the United States until 1868, when MIT established a formal curriculum, followed by Cornell University in 1871 and the University of Illinois in 1873. State laws did not regulate standards or responsibilities, and no common definition of the word "architect" existed when master builders like Kampmann were practicing in Texas. The shingle outside the office could say whatever they wished. It was not until the next generation, starting with Alfred Giles and including James Wahrenberger, James Riely Gordon, Albert Felix Beckmann, and Leo Maria Joseph Dielmann, that the architect as educated thinker was separated from the hands-on builder in America, in the tradition that Vitruvius originally deplored. The following generation of Atlee Ayres and son Robert Ayres, George Willis, and Ralph Cameron was never questioned as to whether they were architects because they were properly credentialed as professionals, by which time there were legal definitions and consequences to the term and its misuse. The term "master builder" no longer had relevance, and "housewright" became a dated term for a carpenter.

In a biography published in 1894, Kampmann (or immediate family members) summarized his accomplishments as changing the city into a more sophisticated one, "so much so that Mr. Kampmann found it advisable to lay aside the pick and trowel, and go into [the] business as a contractor and builder."[14] Kampmann was a man of his time, a multi-talented builder, designer, businessman, and philanthropist, whose name and contribution should be better remembered by the modern city he helped shape.

The skyline and streetscape of San Antonio today are a result of the amalgamation of the distinct Spanish, German, and Anglo traditions. It is the physical expression of the city's favorite celebration and the core of its identity: Fiesta. This is a celebration of San Antonio culture—foods, flowers, Alamo lore, bright colors, music, creative headwear and medals, temporary royalty, *papel picado*, beer and margaritas, *cascarones*, social customs, humor, and self-parody. It is a multi-ethnic and multi-generational party that for ten days every year celebrates the neighborhood and the city, the individual and collective heritage, and serves as a great excuse for a parade—or three.

{ Endnotes }

1. Information on Kampmann's background can be found in *Biographical Encyclopedia of Texas* (New York: Southern Publishing Company, 1880), 51–52; *Memorial and General Record of Southwest Texas* (1894), 657–60; and Frank W. Johnson, *A History of Texans Volume II* (American Historical Society, 1914), 1251–2. These biographical essays were probably written as PR pieces by Kampmann himself, or by his immediate descendants shortly after his death, and became the sources for most future descriptions. They differ in how Kampmann projected his background, depending on the audience. He is variously described as "liberally educated in the best schools and academies in Prussia" (1880, 1914); "a member of a prominent family [. . .] well on his way to a distinguished career as a contractor and architect in Prussia" (1914); and "a self-made man" (1880, 1914). His emigration papers identified him as a "mason" while on later trips to Europe, as late as 1865, he listed himself as a "laborer."

2. See Paul Zucker, "Architectural Education in Nineteenth Century Germany," *Journal of the American Society of Architectural Historians* 2, 3 (July 1942), 6–13.

3. Department of Commerce and Labor Bureau of Statistics, *Industrial Education and Industrial Conditions in Germany* Special Consular Reports Vol. XXXIII (Washington, DC: Government Printing Office, 1905), 61–62. See also Herbert M. Baer, "The Course in Architecture at a German 'Technische Hochshule,'" *The American Architect and Building News* Vol 71 (March 16, 1901), 83–85.

4. Johnson, 1252.

5. Barry Bergdoll, "Ernst Friedrich Zwirner," *Encyclopedia of Architects* (New York: MacMillan, 1982), 477–78.

6. Paul-Georg Custodis, "The Church of St. Apollinaris in Remagen, Germany—Its Significance and Restoration" in Section 3: Conservation; *Conference Proceedings: Strategies for the World's Cultural Heritage. Preservation in a Globalised World: Principles, Practices, and Perspectives* (Icomos, 2002), 137.

7. The better known St. Apollinare in Classe, consecrated in 549, was erected over his grave in Ravenna, Italy.

8. Jukka Jokilehto, *History of Architectural Conservation* (Oxford: Butterworth-Heinemann, 2002), 116–19.

9. The exterior and interior of the Cathedral were both restored again between 1985 and 2003.

10. *Biographical Encyclopedia of Texas* (1880), 52.

11. Commonly referred to as the *Adelsverein,* the official name was the *Verein zum Schltze Deutscher Einwanderer in* Texas or Society for the Protection of German Immigrants in Texas. It was organized by twenty-one noblemen in Germany in 1842 to encourage an organized emigration for the purpose of establishing a new German community in Texas. See Rudolph L. Biesele, *The History of German Settlements in Texas, 1831–1861* (Austin: Von Boeckmann-Jones, 1930); reprinted by Eakin Press 1964 and the German-Texas Heritage Society 1987.

12. See Biesele, 1930; Gilbert G. Benjamin, PhD, "Germans in Texas," in *German American Annals* Vol 7 (1909); and Moritz Tiling, *History of the German Element in Texas from 1820–1850* (Houston, 1913). For a more current assessment, see Mike Rapport, *1848: Year of Revolution* (New York: Basic Books, 2009).

13. *Memorial and Genealogical Record,* 1894, 658.

14. *Biographical Encyclopedia of Texas,* 1880, 52.

15. New Orleans Passenger Lists, 1820–1945.

16. Biographical Encyclopedia of Texas, 1880, 52.

17. Ibid.; Johnson, 1252.

18. S.W. Pease, *They Came to San Antonio,* (privately published, no date, ca. 1940s) 28–29; Dr. Kenneth Bonnet, personal correspondence with author. Philip and Anna's first child, Johann Christian, died in infancy in Charlottenberg. Both Charles and Daniel served as officers in the 1st Texas Cavalry for the Union. Daniel later served as police chief in San Antonio and Sheriff in Bexar County. Peter was killed during the Civil War. John Andrew rose to the rank of sergeant major in the Confederacy, and after being discharged due to injuries, became a tax collector in Maverick County and later served two terms as the county judge. Another son, Wilhelm Jakob (1847–1904), was born in San Antonio.

19. For a contemporary account of hauling, see August Santleben, *A Texas Pioneer* (New York: Neale Publishing) 1910).

20. Gilbert Giddings Benjamin (*The Germans in Texas; A Study in Immigration* (New York: Cornell University) 1909: 104.

21. *Ibid.* 107.

22. *Ibid.* 113.

23. An excellent permanent exhibit demonstrating the types of housing built in various Texas geographies by different ethnic settlers can be experienced at the San Antonio Botanical Garden. The "Texas Native Trail" features regional flora next to authentic relocated houses, including a *jacal*, log cabin, adobe structure, Hill Country *fachwerk* cottages, and others.

CHAPTER TWO

1. Johnson, 1252.

2. US Census, 1860; headstone, San Antonio Cemetery #1.

3. See Pease "John Fries," *They Came to Texas*; Christopher Long, "John M. Fries," *Handbook of Texas Online* (Texas State Historical Association [TSHA]); Bess Carroll, "'The Market House,' Chapter 58, The Story of San Antonio: 300 Years of Romance" in *San Antonio Light*, June 20, 192x (year unclear).

4. Willard Robinson, *Gone From Texas* (College Station, Texas) 1981, quoted in Bess Carroll.

5. Long; Kevin R. Young "Edwin Burr Babbitt," *Handbook of Texas Online* (TSHA).

6. It is possible that the vague references seen frequently to Kampmann's work on the Quartermaster's Depot refers to the Alamo, as no evidence has been found that he worked on the Depot at Fort Sam Houston. According to Frederick C. Chabot, *With the Makers of San Antonio* (privately published) 1937 the Russi, Enderle, Stumberg, and Fries families were all related by marriage.

7. This house looks like Kampmann's work, but there is no evidence that he built it.

8. Stumberg's daughter Lena married Frank W. McAllister, Sr.

9. San Antonio *Light*, September 8, 1884.

10. Roxanne Kuter Williamson, *Austin, Texas; An American Architectural History* (San Antonio: Trinity Press), 1973: 29 fn 11. She also stated that the building was used later to house the Supreme Court and converted during the Civil War to a cap and cartridge factory.

11. Bill Moore, *Bastrop County 1691–1900* (Bastrop County Historical Society, Rev. ed., 1977), 165; Chuck Leonard, AIA, "Visiting Specialist Report on the Bastrop County Courthouse (District Court Room)" prepared for National Register Department of Texas Historical Commission

(THC), commissioned by Texas Historical Commission, April 1983, in Bastrop County Historical Society Vertical Files: Courthouse. See also Texas Historical Records Survey, Inventory of the County Archives of Texas, No 11, Bastrop County, June 1941, 9 cites Minutes of Commissioners Court, entry 1.

12. Moore, 1977, 165; Texas Historical Records Survey, Works Progress Administration (WPA), *Inventory of the County Archives of Texas* No. 11 Bastrop County (San Antonio: The Texas Historical Records Survey, 1941).

13. Leonard, 1983, fn 15 cites *Police Court Records*, Office, County Clerk's Office, Vol A., 232.

14. Kenneth Kessulus, *History of Bastrop County 1846–1865* (Austin: Jenkins Publishing Co, 1987), 53. Note the first Americanization of Kampmann's name using his middle name Herman, dropping the final letter. Later he changed Johann to John as Fries had done.

15. Texas Historical Records Survey, *Inventory of the County Archives of Texas, No 11, Bastrop County*, June 1941, 9.

16. Quoted in Kesselus, 1987, 51; cites *Bexar County Commissioners Court Minutes (BCCCM)* Vol A: 200–3.

17. Kesselus, 1987, 53, cites *BCCCM*, Vol A: 356.

18. *Ibid.* cites *BCCCM*, Vol A: 200–3.

19. Moore, 1977, 165; Kesselus, 1987, 53 quoting the *Gazette*, May 28, 1853.

20. Kesselus, 1987, 53 cites *BCCCM* Vol. A: 356. The ceiling and stairs were not built until 1855, and a lightning rod was added in 1856.

21. Texas Historical Record Survey 1941: 9 fn 64 cites Police Court Record, Vol A: 356.

22. *Ibid,* fn 65 cites Police Court Record, Vol A: 437.

23. Memorial & Genealogical Record, 1894, 658.

24. San Antonio *Express,* May 7, 1914; "Ilse's Personal Story" in possession of Juanita Chipman.

25. *City Council Journal,* City of San Antonio, Texas, 1848 and 1849, cited in Farrell. L. Tucker, "Edifice of Order: San Antonio City Halls and Jails 1731–1915," *Stirpes* 39, 3 (September 1999), 53.

26. *Proceedings of the City Council,* Sept. 2 and Dec. 3, 1851, City Clerk's Office, San Antonio.

27. Sylvia Ann Santos, "Courthouses of Bexar County, 1731–1978" (Bexar County Historical Commission, 1979).

28. San Antonio *Express*, September 28, 1867.

29. Fred Mosebach, "Chrysler's Day in Court Recalls His Role of Cadi in Old Bat Cave," San Antonio *Express,* October 27, 1935.

30. Ed Froboese, "And I Remember When—", *San Antonio Light,* May 1, 1933.

31. Tucker, 57.
32. Tucker, 58.
33. Lawrence Phillip Knight, "Becoming a City and Becoming American; San Antonio, Texas, 1848–1861," (PhD Diss. Texas A&M, 1997), 33; Pease, 133.
34. Chabot, 384; Knight, 1997, 32–33.
35. Cecelia Steinfeldt *San Antonio Was: Seen Through a Magic Lantern* (San Antonio Museum Association 1978), 158.
36. *Ibid*, 162, fig 175.
37. *Ibid*, 158–60; San Antonio *Express,* March 8, 1884, reprinted in Donald E. Everett, *San Antonio, The Flavor of Its Past* (San Antonio: Trinity University, 1975), 125.
38. "Buckhorn Saloon Origins," San Antonio *Express,* March 8, 1884, reprinted in Everett (1975), 125.
39. Pease, 133; San Antonio *Express,* September 1, 1895, reprinted in Everett, 1975, 114.
40. Steinfeldt, 1978, 158–60; "Buckhorn Saloon Origins," San Antonio *Express,* March 8, 1884 reprinted in Everett, 1975, 125; San Antonio *Express,* September 1, 1895 reprinted in Everett *Flavor* 1975, 114.
41. "An Old Landmark Gone," San Antonio *Daily Express,* February 23, 1902.
42. Fries is inconsistently credited as a designer. Often he was a builder and his role in the design phase is unclear. For example, the Vance House is credited to Fries alone, but the Market House architect was John Campbell, while Fries and Rossi were construction engineers, according to Cecilia Steinfeldt (78), while newspaper accounts at the time of its demolition in the 1920s credited Fries. The destruction of this building was one of the events leading to the founding of the San Antonio Conservation Society. The façade was said to be the inspiration for the new San Pedro Playhouse, built in 1930 by Bartlett Cocke and Marvin Eickenroht.
43. Kenneth W. Wheeler, *To Wear a City's Crown: The Beginnings of Urban Growth in Texas, 1836–1865* (Cambridge: Harvard University Press, 1968), 127.
44. San Antonio *Express,* June 30, 1935.
45. Raymond Boryczka, "The Busiest Man in Town: John Hermann Kampmann and the Urbanization of San Antonio, Texas, 1884–1885," *Southwestern Historical Quarterly* [SHQ] 115, 4, April 2012, 333.
46. 1850 Federal Census; Kent Keeth, "Sankt Antonius: Germany in the Alamo City of the 1850s," *SHQ* 76 (Oct. 1972), 201.

CHAPTER THREE

1. William A. McClintock, "Through Texas and Northern Mexico in 1846–1847," *Southwestern Historical Quarterly,* 34, 2 (October 1930), 147.

2. Frederick Law Olmsted, *A Journey Through Texas; or, A Winter of Saddle and Camp Life on the Border Country of the United States and Mexico* (London: Sampson Low, Son & Co., 1857), 149.

3. The name was spelled both Eager and Eagar, often within the same document.

4. See Terry Jordan, "A Gabled Folk House of the Mexico/Texas Borderland," (unpublished, ca. 1980).

5. In 1875, son John Herff married the Kampmanns' daughter Eda. See Juanita Herff Drought Chipman, *The Passing of Gifts* (Bloomington, In: Xlibris, 2011), 49.

6. Penelope Borden, "'The Bright Shawl,' Colorful 'Mantle of Charity' The Junior League Will Spread in San Antonio," San Antonio *Express,* March 21, 1926.

7. See Charles R. Porter, Jr., *Spanish Water, Anglo Water: Early Development in San Antonio* (College Station: Texas A&M Press, 2009), 92.

8. *Bexar County Deed Records M,* 150, cited in I. Wayne Cox, Anne A. Fox, and Steve A. Tomka, "Archaeological Background, Museum Reach," San Antonio River Improvements Project (UTSA Center for Archaeological Research, 2002), 9; Tucker, 54, citing Vinton Lee James, *Frontier and Pioneer Recollections,* suggests that the land might have been sold to finance the new courthouse/jail known as the "Bat Cave" built by Kampmann and Fries (see chapter 2).

9. See chapter 6 for further discussion of the San Antonio Water Works Company and Kampmann's role in it.

10. "Realty Prices 25 Years Ago Are Modest Now," San Antonio *Express,* October 26, 1922.

11. "Francis Louis des Mazieres Store Building & House, Martinez and South Alamo Streets, San Antonio, Bexar County, TX" (Historic American Buildings Survey [HABS] TX-33-A-2, 1934).

12. *Ibid.*

13. *Ibid.*

14. "Three Old Homes in San Antonio Marked for Study," San Antonio *Express,* January 21, 1934, 1-2 A.

15. HABS documentation, 1934.

16. "Ancient House Held First Bathtub," San Antonio *Light,* September 9, 1929. Article erroneously dates the house to 1830s/early '40s, "the early days of San Antonio."

17. HABS Drawings/photos/desc #33-A-2, 1934/36.

18. "Long Life No Chore to Native San Antonian," San Antonio *Light,* February 19, 1940.
19. San Antonio *Light,* September 9, 1929.
20. HABS documentation, 1934.
21. HABS documentation, 1934.
22. The contract between A[urelia] W. Dashiell and J.H. Kampmann was not signed until August 6, 1856. The house was to be completed by November 30, 1856, at a cost of $3,250, according to Bexar County Records, 1856, Vol 1, # 326, 329–330.
23. Letter from Jeremiah Dashiell to his daughter dated June 22, 1856, in San Antonio Conservation Society (SACS) Vertical file.
24. James Garner, author of the HABS notes, called it "prestigious"; Cecilia Steinfeldt referred to it as "pretentious".
25. "The Old Slave Dead," San Antonio *Light,* November 17, 1883.
26. Steinfeldt, 1978, 152; HABS documentation: 1968: 4.
27. HABS, 3.
28. Paula Allen quoting SACS Yearbook in "Dashiell House Sits Near the Heart of La Villita" San Antonio *Express* Feb. 25, 2001.
29. Lewis T. Fisher, *Saving San Antonio: The Precarious Preservation of a Heritage* (Lubboch:Texas Tech University Press, 1996), 199; 221.
30. NIOSA is "A Night in Old San Antonio," the main event sponsored by the San Antonio Conservation Society in La Villita for three nights during Fiesta Week. The proceeds finance much of the budget of the organization for the following year.
31. "Beckmann Family Papers," Daughters of the Republic of Texas Collection, Col 10931, 2001. According to Chabot, the Beckmanns were likely the first German family to settle permanently in San Antonio in May, 1846 (1937: 375).
32. Pease, 17; "John Beckmann Pioneer Is Dead," San Antonio *Gazette,* April 12, 1907.
33. Vinton L. James, 146; obituary, 1907.
34. Steinfeldt, 164.
35. Wayne Cox, "Archaeological Monitoring for the Casa Rio Restaurant Expansion, San Antonio" (UTSA: Center for Archaeological Research) 1992: 4.
36. Their son Albert Beckmann (1855–1900) was a well-known architect and partner of James Wahrenberger. When he died, his pallbearers included Kampmann's friends and clients A.F. Staacke, F. A. Hummel, and Henry Baetz. Beckmann, Joseph Baetz, and Charles Hummel had been close friends.
37. Cox, "Casa Rio," (1992), 5.

38. Cox, 1992, 5–6.

39. San Antonio folklore holds that the reason Menger built the hotel was to put up visitors who came to his brewery. San Antonio *Light,* May 31, 1929. At any rate, the brewery was the literal foundation for the hotel.

40. Michael C. Hennech and Tracé Etienne-Gray, "Brewing Industry," *Handbook of Texas Online [HTO].*

41. "SA Beneficiary Association," San Antonio *Daily Light,* November 9, 1895.

42. Degen was so well known in the community that following his death, a stone carver made a bust of him to show off his skill to potential clients, who immediately recognized the late Mr. Degen because he had been such a fixture in San Antonio. "Stone Carver Produces Fine Clay Model: Rudolph Oerter Makes Remarkably Lifelike Bust of Late Chas. P. Degen," San Antonio *Light,* May 12, 1912.

43. Theresa Gold, "Charles & Elizabeth Degen," *Our Heritage* 34, 4 (Summer 1993), 36.

44. Daughter Anna L. Degen married John Fries's son Fred.

45. Bess Carroll, "Famous Brew Recalled as Birthplace Re-Opens," San Antonio *Light,* May 31, 1929.

46. Quoted in Fred Mosebach, "Early Breweries Tell Interesting Story of Beer That Made San Antonio Famous," San Antonio *Express,* August 25, 1935.

47. *Our Heritage* 34,3 (Spring 1993), 27. Degen's beer won a first-place medal at the St. Louis World's Fair in 1904.

48. Anne A. Fox and Marcie Renner, eds., *Historical and Archaeological Investigations at the Site of Rivercenter Mall (Las Tiendas), San Antonio, Texas* (UTSA Center for Archaeological Research [CAR] No. 270 ,1999), 18—cites Ramsdell 1945.

49. *Ibid.,* 21.

50. Part of the folklore of San Antonio is that the house was built by William Riddle as a wedding present for his daughter Sarah. But William Riddle died in 1847 (before Kampmann's arrival in San Antonio and when Sarah was five years old). The contract dated 1869 is signed by Robert and Sarah.

51. When South Alamo Street was widened, the house became much closer to the street.

52. The 1900 Federal Census lists Sarah, 59; twin daughters Florence and Blanche, 32; Blanche's husband Francis Badger, 38, and two children, ages 8 and 5; Sarah's mother Elizabeth Canterbury, 80; a boarder; and Mary, a long-time servant. Sarah's granddaughter Aline Badger Carter served as Poet Laureate of Texas from 1947–49, and was the mother of attorney David Carter.

CHAPTER FOUR

1. "Nearly a Half Century Old: Sketch of the Casino Association From its Birth," unknown source ca. 1890, found in Mrs. Josephine Broadbent's Scrapbook 1905 at the Institute for Texan Cultures (ITC).
2. Charles Ramsdell, "The Glamorous Casino," June 20, 1948, unidentified clipping in ITC files, reprinted in Charles Ramsdell, *San Antonio: A Historical and Pictorial Guide* (Austin: University of Texas Press, 1959), 1985.
3. This was probably the same building referred to earlier as on Presa St., one block east. At some point Kampmann acquired ownership of the building. According to an unidentified newspaper clipping ca 1900, the estate planned on tearing down "the old landmark, [on a lot that extended back to Crockett] placing in its stead a building of modern design."
4. Casino Club Holds Jubilee Demonstration," unidentified clipping, November 11, 1904, ITC.
5. Skat was a popular nineteenth-century card game. Club records indicate that occasionally, members had to be reminded to pay up past wagers. The July 13, 1872, board minutes included a reprimand for certain members' lack of interest in club affairs other than skat.
6. Pearson Newcomb, *Alamo City,* (San Antonio: Pearson Newcomb, 1926), 75; Vinton E. James, "Recollections," San Antonio *Express,* December 31, 1933.
7. Obituary, San Antonio *Express,* April 13, 1907.
8. San Antonio *Express,* June 14, 1924.
9. Patricia Hillert, "Old Casino Club Was Hub," San Antonio *Light* February 5, 1950.
10. San Antonio *Light,* January 6, 1907.
11. Some years later Kampmann was hired to build the first vaudeville or "Dingle Dangle" theater on Alamo Plaza. Thinking it was a theater like the Casino Hall, he requested reserved seats for himself and his family for opening night. It was then explained to him that it was a slang term for a "girlie show," and respectable married women would never patronize such an establishment. V. L. James, "Old Times in San Antonio," *Frontier Times* 6, 9 (June 1929), 379.
12. Charles Ramsdell, "Old England in Bexar," San Antonio *Express* magazine, July 18, 1948. There are also reports that Thielepape was the architect instead of Fries.
13. Hillert, 1950; Adel Speiser, *The Story of the Theatre in San Antonio* (Thesis, 1948), 21–5; "City's Oldest Club," San Antonio *Express,* February 24, 1924.
14. Hillert, 1950.
15. Quoted in Hillert, 1950.

16. "Nearly a Half Century Old," ca 1890.

17. "City's Oldest Club," 1924.

18. *Ibid.*

19. Kampmann was one of the original directors when the club was organized in December, 1881.

20. San Antonio *Herald,* August 31, 1858.

21. Sylvia Ann Santos, "Courthouses of Bexar County 1731–1978," (SA: Bexar County Historical Commission, 1979).

22. "Monument of Determination, Foresight," San Antonio *Light,* December 18, 1966.

23. From the minutes of the first general meeting, quoted in San Antonio *Light,* December 18, 1966.

24. *Ibid.*

25. Mary Mathis El-Beheri and Susan Clayton, "High School Students Research History of German-English School in San Antonio," *Die Unterrichtspraxis/Teaching German* 8, 2 (Autumn 1975), 64.

26. Mary Clark, "German-English School of San Antonio," *Texas History,* March 1980, 7; San Antonio *Express,* June 9, 1936.

27. Students and alumni included members of the Guenther, Frank, Degen, Horn, Peltzer, Heuermann, Hoerner, Wulff, Groos, Baetz, Steves, Elmendorf, Zork, Heusinger, Canterbury, Rhodius, Maverick, Terrell, Vance, Eagar, Herff, Griesenbeck, Kampmann, Hertzberg, Hummel, McAllister, Fries, Wurzbach, Oppenheimer, and Hugo families.

28. Ms. El-Beheri's fourth-year German class at MacArthur High School in San Antonio researched and translated original documents in German, including the minutes of the Board of Directors at the DRT Library at the Alamo, to learn what they could about this school and its founders. Riotte, president of the board from 1858–60, left Texas in 1861 because he was a Union loyalist. Berens, who ran the school from 1858–74, served as principal and teacher. He owned a book-store in town, was manager of the *Krankenkassen Verein,* and was elected to the Texas Legislature; he retired to Switzerland in 1875. Nette was the first pharmacist in San Antonio; Thielepape was an artist, architect, bookkeeper, founder of the *Männerchor,* and two-term mayor of San Antonio. Friesleben served as the first elected city engineer (1857–65) and surveyed much of the city. Theissen was a merchant and alderman.

29. Steinfeldt, 146 per Dr. Jane F. Baskin, "German-English Pupils to Hold Fourth Reunion," Ben Wise Scrapbook, 127 in DRT Library at the Alamo.

30. Clark, 1980: 7; Baskin, 1928.

31. Hillert, 1951; Clark, 1980.

32. Patricia Hillert, "School Ends After 90 Years," unidentified newspaper, June 24, 1951.

33. "Will Try to Save It," San Antonio *Light,* October 11, 1887.

34. Homer H. Lansberry, "Menger Hotel," Historical and Descriptive Material (HABS) TEX-35, July 26, 1937: 2.

35. Steinfeldt, 1978,120; fn 44 cites Sam Woolford, "Menger Hotel," San Antonio *Light,* February 1, 1959.

36. Docia Schultz Williams, *The History and Mystery of the Menger Hotel* (Dallas: Republic of Texas Press, 2000).

37. San Antonio *Herald,* January 18, 1859 quoted in Williams, 2000, 8.

38. Quoted in Williams, 10.

39. Homer H. Lansberry, "Menger Hotel Data Pages," HABS No. Tex-35, 1936.

40. "When, And If, Bombs Fall Upon S. A.," San Antonio *Light,* December 29, 1940: 1.

41. Timothy Draves, "Mary Menger (1816–1887)," *The Journal of Life and Culture of San Antonio,* University of the Incarnate Word online publication http://www.uiw.edu/sanantonio/draves.html (accessed October 18, 2006).

42. Hennech and Etienne-Gray.

43. Glen Lich, *The German Texasns* (San Antonio: Institute of Texan Cultures, 1981; revised 1996).

44. "Menger Family Archives Record Army's History," San Antonio *Express,* November 26, 1940. Fort Sam Houston was built on land donated by the city as well as private citizens, including Caroline Kampmann.

45. Williams, 30.

46. Stephen Gould, *The Alamo City Guide,* (New York: Macgowan & Slipper Printers, 1882), 134.

47. It is a long-held legend that Carrie Nation's hatchet marks can be seen in the solid cherry bar, but it is unlikely. According to Sam Woolford, she visited the Menger Bar on the afternoon of January 8, 1908, sans hatchet. The San Antonio *Light* posted the following bulletin on the front page: "At 3 o'clock, the police department stated that Mrs. Nation would be allowed all the liberties of the city, but that she would not be allowed to break any furniture as the saloon men in this city pay their taxes."(561-62). Sam Woolford "Carrie Nation in Texas" *Southwestern Historical Quarterly* Vol 63, April 1960: 557-64.

48. Bartee Haile, "This Week in Texas History," *Lone Star Iconoclast,* January 31, 2006.

49. Williams, 35.

50. Haile, 2006.
51. *Ibid.*
52. Clayton Stapleton, "The Menger Hotel," July 17, 2004.
53. Williams, 2000, 14.
54. Draves, 2006.
55. Frederic C. Chabot, "St. Joseph's—Monument to Indomitable Spirit of German Pioneers," San Antonio *Express,* May 26, 1935; "St. Joseph's Downtown Church: A History of St. Joseph Church Founded by German-Speaking Catholics in 1868," (San Antonio: St. Joseph's), 2.
56. The steeple, completed in 1898, was designed by James Wahrenberger.
57. Theresa Gold, "St. Joseph's Celebrates 125 Years in San Antonio," unknown source, 1993.
58. Frederick C. Chabot, "Methodists the First to Bring Protestantism Into Texas," San Antonio *Express,* February 24, 1935.
59. Garland Crook, 1964, 95–96, 235.
60. Fragments of letters between Upjohn and Fish dating to 1859 have been found, but other than that, it is not clear how Upjohn secured the commission. It is known that Upjohn and Rev. John F. Fish, a US Army chaplain stationed in San Antonio in 1849, were both members of the New York Ecclesiological Society formed in 1848, and there was a tightly knit Episcopalian community among the military stationed in San Antonio. National Register Nomination, 1998; Lewis Fisher, *Saint Mark's Episcopal Church: 150 Years of Ministry in Downtown San Antoni*o (San Antonio: Maverick Publishing) 2008, 10.
61. San Antonio *Herald,* August 9, 1973, per Fisher, 2008, 125.
62. It has since been moved twice.
63. National Register Nomination (NR), 1998.
64. He bore the title "Dean" during the time that St. Mark's was designated the Cathedral of the Missionary District of Western Texas from 1876–1888.
65. NR 1998.
66. As late as 1880, he was describing himself as Catholic, while Caroline "was a communicant of [St. Mark's] from the day of the first service in the structure [1875]" according to her obituary in the San Antonio *Light,* May 7, 1914.
67. Charles Bertrand, HABS Documentation, 1936.
68. NR 1998.
69. Fisher, 2008, 24.
70. San Antonio AIA (SAAIA) Chapter, *Guide to San Antonio Architecture* (1986), 42.
71. Ramsdell, "Old England," 1948. Richardson is buried under the chancel.

Charles Bertrand, HABS documentation, December 3, 1936, from information in an article by Frederick C. Chabot in the San Antonio *Express,* March 3, 1935 [sic] date should be February 24, 1935.

72. Ramsdell, 1948.
73. Ramsdell, 1948.
74. SAAIA, 1986, 42.
75. Bertrand, HABS, 1936.
76. Abe Levy, "St. Mark's Recaptures Its History," San Antonio *Express,* January 12, 2013.
77. Pease, 153.
78. Personal correspondence with Dr. Kenneth Bonnet, March 2013.
79. Raymond Boryczka, "'The Busiest Man in Town': John Hermann Kampmann and the Urbanization of San Antonio, Texas, 1848–1885," *Southwestern Historical Quarterly* 115, 4 (April 2012), 339.
80. *Biographical Encyclopedia of Texas* 1880, 52; Pease, 156; Boryczka says they were originally organized to support the Union.
81. War record.
82. *Memorial and Genealogical Records,* 1894, 658.
83. Garner, 1969, 2–3; W.W. Campbell: Ward 3 alderman July 1, 1857–January 1, 1858; January 1, 1859–January 2, 1862.
84. L. Engelke, "Old Arsenal Served Army for 85 Years," San Antonio *Express,* November 14, 1965. 1965 cited in Chumney Report.
85. Wesley Shank, "HABS Architectural Report," 1968.
86. *Ibid.*
87. "San Antonio Arsenal Historical Report, 1919–1942," SAA File No. 314.7 copy in San Antonio Conservation Society Vertical Files.
88. *Ibid.*
89. Texas State Historical Marker #212, 1977.
90. "History of the San Antonio Arsenal," paper given at San Antonio Conservation Society, Feb. 10, 1956, cited in Victor and Victor Consultants, Inc. Historical Report done for Chumney/Urrutia, 1985.
91. San Antonio *Light,* November 7, 1920.
92. "San Antonio Arsenals Through Two Centuries," San Antonio *Express,* December 8, 1931; "San Antonio Arsenal Passes It's [sic] Sixty-first Birthday Anniversary," San Antonio *Light,* November 7, 1920.
93. Stephen Gould, 1882, 52.
94. Texas State Historical Marker #212, 1977.
95. L. Engelke, "Old Arsenal Serving Army for 85 Years," San Antonio *Express,* November 14, 1965.
96. War Records.

97. Reprinted in the Galveston *Weekly News,* November 9, 1864.
98. *Memorial and Genealogical Record,* 658.
99. Facsimile of document accompanied by facsimile of oath affidavit.

CHAPTER FIVE

1. "Confederate Photo Maker [David Perry Barr] Leaves Plates Recalling City's Early Day Leaders," San Antonio *Evening News,* May 1, 1925 (includes a portrait of Kampmann).
2. Steinfeldt, 1978, 163.
3. Details about the house are primarily from the HABS photographs and description, Project Number Tex-396, completed in 1937 by Homer H. Lansberry and Bartlett Cocke, based on information provided by August Herff, architect and great-grandson who lived next door.
4. Morrison, 1890, 100.
5. John and Caroline Kampmann's grandson John Bennett Herff moved in with his new bride Florence Harris in 1902. Their daughters were all born in the house: Carolyn Kampmann Herff [Herff], 1904; Ilse Herff [Frost], 1906; and Jean Herff [Henderson], 1910. Carolyn's daughters Juanita and Caroline recall playing in the house as children.
6. Steinfeldt, 1978, 164.
7. San Antonio *Herald,* January 12, 1872.
8. Borden, 1926.
9. *Ibid.*
10. *Ibid.*
11. San Antonio *City Directories,* 1880s.
12. Corner.
13. San Antonio *Express,* unknown date.
14. Fred Mosebach, "Many Changes Mark Stride of Meat Industry Since Days of Old Market House," San Antonio *Express,* July 15, 1934.
15. *Memorial and Genealogical Record,* 1894, 658.
16. 1877–78 *San Antonio City Directory* lists J.H. Kampmann as a contractor and his son Hermann as clerk.
17. Brent Hull, *Historic Millwork,* (New York: John Wiley & Sons, 2003), 1.
18. 238*Ibid.,* xiii.
19. Charles G. Boelhauwe (1848–1924) came from Germany in 1869 and worked in his uncle John Kampmann's mill with his brother Joseph T. Boelhauwe (1845–1922). They were sons of Theodore and Agnes Kampmann Boelhauwe. Charles went on to become a contractor and built the Masonic Temple in 1907 and the Crockett Hotel in 1909. Joseph immigrated to San Antonio in 1874 and worked in Kampmann's mill for about eighteen months before helping build the first railroad to San Antonio in 1877, the Galveston,

Harrisburg, and San Antonio, and was inspector of masonry of that railway; he was elected Ward 5 alderman from 1891–93. Their sister Bernadine married Louis William Menger, son of the hotel founders. Charles's son Charles T. Boelhauwe (1886–1977) became an architect, partnering with Sanguinet and Staats from 1918–19 on the Burns Building on Houston Street.

20. Chabot, 1937, 381; "Groos Bank Active Participant in 100 Years of South Texas Growth," San Antonio *Express*, February 28, 1954; Clarence La-Roche, "Germans Pioneered HemisFair Site Area," San Antonio *Express*, February 6, 1965. Giles's building was replaced in 1929.

21. In 1982, Groos National Bank was purchased by Tom Benson, who established Benson Financial Corp., later sold to Norwest Banks.

22. Lillie May Hagner, *Alluring San Antonio: Through the Eyes of an Artist*, (San Antonio: The Naylor Company, 1940), 49–50.

23. Tulitas Jamieson, *Tulitas of Torreon: Reminiscences of Life in Mexico as Told to Evelyn Payne*, (El Paso, 1969), 5 quoted in Steinfeldt, 166.

24. Fisher, 1996, 377.

25. Mary Carolyn Hollers Jutson [George], *Alfred Giles: An English Architect in Texas and Mexico* (San Antonio: Trinity University Press, 1972). She cites Giles's daughter Marcella Booth as stating that "while Giles was in Kampmann's employ, he was anxious to go into business for himself, but each attempt at resigning from the Kampmann firm was countered by the offer of a substantial increase in salary" resulting in "considerable animosity" when Giles did make the break after three years, although they continued to work together.

26. *Ibid.*, 48.

27. Information on Halffs from Patrick Dearen, *Halff of Texas* (Austin, TX: Eakin Press, 2000). See also Natalie Ornish, "The Ranchers" in *Pioneer Jewish Texans: Their Impact on Texas and American History for Four Hundred Years 1590–1990* (Dallas: Texas Heritage Press, 1989), Chapter 5.

28. Dearen, 81.

29. Their son Godchaux A.C. Halff (1877–1950) founded WOAI radio in San Antonio in 1922.

30. San Antonio *Express,* May 30, 1905.

31. Dan Oppenheimer, *D. & A. Oppenheimer, Bankers (Unincorporated): Transcribed Interviews with Mr. Dan Oppenheimer*, Interviews conducted by Larry Meyer (Austin: University of Texas, 1971), 5–6. The interviewee was Daniel Oppenheimer's grandson.

32. One of their daughters, Alma Oppenheimer, married Alexander Halff, and son Jesse Daniel Oppenheimer married Mayer Halff's daughter Lillie. The Halffs and the Oppenheimers were both prominent members of the San Antonio Jewish community.

33. "A Splendid Residence," San Antonio *Express,* October 25, 1878.
34. *Ibid.*
35. Deed, May 18, 1875.
36. San Antonio *Express,* April 19, 1925, quoted in Donald E. Everett, *San Antonio's Monte Vista: Architecture and Society in a Gilded Age* (San Antonio: Maverick Publishing, 1999), 85.
37. James David Carter (ed.), *The First Century of Scottish Rite Masonry in Texas, 1867–1967,* (Waco: The Scottish Rite Bodies, 1967), 304–5.
38. "Big Celebration Will Mark Opening of New Citadel," San Antonio *Light,* June 25, 1920.
39. Bonnie Sue Jacobs, "Ancestral Gift Preserved," San Antonio *Express,* May 25, 1972.
40. San Antonio *Daily Express,* September 16, 1881.
41. Quoted in George, 1972, 53.
42. Eda Herff's Diary, March 1884 as translated from the Steilschrift dialect by Rudolf Scheffrahn (2003), 16–17, in possession of Juanita Herff Chipman.
43. San Antonio was a small town socially. Joseph Baetz was a member of the Casino Club and the Volunteer Fire Department with Kampmann. His daughter Amelia Baetz married Henry Elmendorf (future mayor of San Antonio and brother of Emily Elmendorf, who was Gus Kampmann's first wife). Daughter Fanny Baetz married future mayor Albert Steves, son of Edward Steves, who commissioned the Steves House.
44. The stone wall of the original Staacke Building remains behind James Reilly Gordon's new façade built in 1890 for Staacke & Sons. Kampmann may also have built a house for August F. Staacke on Commerce.

CHAPTER SIX

1. Alexander Joske, "San Antonio, the Beautiful City, One of the Prettiest Cities I Know of in This Country," San Antonio *Express,* June 17, 1923.
2. San Antonio *Express,* August 30, 1877; Caroline Remy, "A Study of Transition: San Antonio From a Frontier to an Urban Community 1875–1900" (MA Thesis, Trinity, 1960), 55, 80–1.
3. Obituary, San Antonio *Express,* September 8, 1885.
4. *Evening Light,* March 18, 1883; "Defiling the Alamo Ditch," San Antonio *Light,* August 20, 1883.
5. "The Alamo Plaza," San Antonio *Evening Light,* April 7, 1882; "The Plaza Fountains," San Antonio *Light,* May 26, 1882.
6. John T. Dickinson (comp.), "Report on the Construction of the Temporary State Capitol at Austin, Texas," 1883.
7. The City Clerk's Office says this bridge was built in 1880. Ray Boryczka cites

Frank Jennings for evidence of its 1860 construction and 1861 and 1868 contracts with Kampmann.

8. Frank W. Jennings, *San Antonio: Story of an Enchanted City* (San Antonio: San Antonio Museum of Art, 1998).

9. San Antonio *Herald*, March 6, 1866; San Antonio *Express*, 1867; San Antonio *Express*, July 2, 1868. Kampmann had a history of bad driving. The San Antonio *Express* reported on July 25, 1869, that "Mr. J.H. Kampmann, it seems, infuses energy into everything he touches, his gentle old buggy horse became so energetic under the touch of its energetic driver on Friday evening, that he ran off, tearing down Main Street, and finally bringing up in front of Stumberg's on Alamo square, smashing the buggy, but fortunately not hurting the occupant."

10. Texas State Historic Marker; Sanborn Map.

11. Stephen Gould, 1882, 118.

12. Cited in Raymond Kresba, "A History of Douglass Academy" (SAISD, 2008), 5.

13. The new school evolved into Douglass High School and then Douglass Junior High School. Douglass Academy, as it was renamed in 2004, was refurbished to serve pre-Kindergarten through fifth grade.

14. "Scientific Society to Celebrate 500th Meeting Tuesday Evening Next," San Antonio *Express*, February 5, 1933; "From the Service of the Scientific Societies," San Antonio *Express*, October 5, 1930. These accounts differ slightly in details; Gammel, *The Laws of Texas, 1822–1897*, 137.

15. Quoted in Rena Maverick Green, ed., *Memoirs of Mary A. Maverick* (San Antonio: Alamo Printing Co., 1921), 133.

16. Quoted in Edwin Mims, *A Biography of Sidney Lanier* (Project Gutenberg, 1998), 70.

17. Vinton L. James, "Old Times in San Antonio," *Frontier Times* 6, 10 (July 1929), 412.

18. San Antonio *Light*, July 2, 1883.

19. James, 412.

20. "Scientific Society to Celebrate," San Antonio *Express*, February 5, 1933.

21. *Ibid.*; Chabot, 412. This became the foundation of the San Antonio Public Library. In 1903, Caroline Kampmann donated land at Market and Presa, where with fifty thousand dollars from Andrew Carnegie, the Carnegie Library was built.

22. Chabot, 388. The property was estimated to be worth one million dollars according to Vinton L. James.

23. Solon K. Stewart, "Fire! Fire! When the Firebell Rang in San Antonio and the Volunteers Responded," San Antonio *Express*, September 10, 1911.

24. *Ibid.*

25. *Ibid.*
26. Fred Mosebach, "Old Engine House Brings Happy Memories of Old San Antonio," San Antonio *Express*, March 24, 1935.
27. Shirley Lerner, "Fire Department History 1848 to 1900," (UTSA) May 13, 1986, posted online at www.safirefighters.com.
28. See Lerner.
29. The Constitution also allowed counties to remand "all persons committing petty offences in the county [...] to such Manual Labor Poor Houses for correction and employment," thus underscoring the historic link between poverty and criminality. Counties tended to build poor farms while cities built poorhouses similar to the traditional almshouse found in the East. See Debbie Mauldin Cottrell, "The County Poor Farm System in Taxes, *Southwest Historical Quarterly* 93,2 (October 1989), 169–90.
30. Cottrell, 174–6.
31. Later San Antonio newspaper accounts tell of efforts to relocate the poorhouse to less valuable real estate, which required removing the bodies from the cemetery.
32. The Gas Company was paying dividends of eight percent by 1882.
33. *Memorial and Genealogical Record* (Chicago: Goodspeed Brothers, 1894), 659. In 1888, the directors elected Friedrich Groos president. Hermann Kampmann was selected as treasurer and then president and general manager.
34. "The Gas Company," San Antonio *Light*, December 17, 1887.
35. Vinton Lee James, 1938, 104.
36. John Fries was appointed manager in 1858. Kampmann carefully selected the site for his home and mill over the Acéquia Madre to ensure fresh water. Refer to the 1883 Ditch Dispute earlier in this chapter.
37. "San Antonio Water Supply Co.," San Antonio *Light and Gazette*, n.d.; Bess Carroll, "History of Water Supply Reveals City's Romance," San Antonio *Light*, September 21, 1924; "Water Company Organized in San Antonio 63 Years Ago," San Antonio *Express*, November 26, 1940. See also Charles R. Porter, Jr., *Spanish Water, Anglo Water* (College Station: Texas A&M University Press), 2009.
38. "News Notes and Comments," San Antonio *Evening Light*, November 20, 1882, 2.
39. "Desirable Citizens," San Antonio *Light*, August 7, 1883.
40. Hennech and Etienne-Gray, "Brewing Industry."
41. "Lone Star Brewing Company," San Antonio *Light*, December 20, 1886.
42. Description from "Lone Star Brewery," San Antonio *Light*, September 18, 1884. Gosling was killed five months later by outlaws Charles Yeager and

James Pitts during an escape attempt as the marshal was escorting them to San Antonio to serve life sentences for robbery.

43. "Lone Star Brewers," San Antonio *Express,* July 13, 1886. The Fashion Theatre was a vaudeville theatre located on Military Plaza. They had a house brass band that paraded through the plaza each day to drum up business.

44. The enlarged campus was listed on the National Register of Historic Places in 1979.

45. "The Lone Star Brewery," San Antonio *Light,* December 22, 1884.

46. Frank Jennings, 261.

47. Cited in National Register nomination form, 1972.

48. Hennech and Etienne-Gray.

49. During Prohibition, Lone Star manufactured Tango, a nonalcoholic beverage.

50. Jennings, 1998, 210.

51. Steinfeldt, 1978, 105.

52. When Kampmann died in 1885, son Hermann acquired his financial interest, but the name of the bank returned to Lockwood Bank. They moved to new headquarters at 201 W. Commerce. The new building, considered the most elaborate in the city when it was new, was torn down in 1914 when the streets were widened. Lockwood retired in 1907, and the bank moved again. In 1918, Lockwood National Bank christened their new Greek Revival bank building at 113 Avenue C (Broadway), next door to the old Fire Station. In 1928, Lockwood National merged with Frost National to create Frost National Bank.

53. This was not the first nor the only four-story building in the city—Francois Giraud's St. Mary's College (La Mansion del Rio Hotel) was built in 1867. The main building of the Lone Star Brewery was also four stories. The Maverick Bank was five stories. But this was the first solid rock (not wood) commercial office building in the center of downtown of that stature and with the expected amenities and prestigious tenants.

54. "The Kampmann Building," San Antonio *Light,* December 22, 1884.

55. Fred Mosebach, "Old Landmarks Vanish in Path of Building Progress," San Antonio *Express,* March 3, 1935.

56. "J.H. Kampmann: The First Enterprising Builder of San Antonio," San Antonio *Light,* September 11, 1884, translated from the *Freie Press,* September 8, 1884.

57. San Antonio *Light,* December 22, 1884.

58. "J.H. Kampmann: Progress and Prosperity of San Antonio," San Antonio *Express,* September 10, 1884.

59. *Ibid.*

60. *Ibid.*
61. Mosebach, 1935.
62. Mosebach, 1935; Edward W. Heusinger, *A Chronology of Events in SA: Being a Concise History of the City Year by Year from the Beginning of its Establishment to the End of the First Half of the 20th Century* (San Antonio, 1951), 51.
63. Mosebach, 1935.
64. Quoted in *Memorial and Genealogical Record,* 1894, 659.

CHAPTER SEVEN

1. *Memorial and Genealogical Record,* 1894, 659.
2. "Famed Ranch Now Playground of Tired Businessman," San Antonio *Express,* November 30, 1924. The land was purchased by the National Golf Association from Kampmann's daughter, Eda, for one hundred thousand dollars and the course was built in record time for an additional eighty-five thousand dollars. It was announced that Atlee Ayres would remodel the old Kampmann ranchhouse into a clubhouse, but that did not come to pass. The course was eventually purchased by the city and became the site of Freeman Coliseum.
3. Galveston *Daily News,* September 8, 1885; San Antonio *Express,* September 8, 1885.
4. Details from "Funeral of Major J.H. Kampmann," San Antonio *Express,* September 15, 1885.
5. "Death Comes to Pioneer Woman Who Leaves Estate Estimated at a Million," San Antonio *Express,* May 17, 1914; "Body to Rest Beside That of Husband," San Antonio *Light,* May 7, 1914.
6. Both Ida and granddaughter Ilse kept diaries about their lives, which are in the possession of Ilse's niece, Juanita Herff Chipman.
7. According to the San Antonio *Light* of September 28, 1886, Hermann was one of the fourteen wealthiest men in the city, with an estimated wealth of eight hundred fifty thousand dollars.
8. Regina and Allen Kosub, "Mackey Brick and Tile: Nelson Mackey Comes to Calaveras," *Wilson County News,* June 8, 2010. Gus was a rebellious son who didn't really want to go into the family business. His father was much closer to Hermann and Ida and was, in fact, often embarrassed by Gus. The final blow was probably when John, "most reluctantly and with feelings of deepest sorrow" but quite publically wrote Gus out of his will for "the dissolute life, which my said son has been and is now leading, and his persistency in such life after the most solemn admonitions from his mother and myself. [...] May God grant that he see the error of his ways and become a good husband and father as well as a dutiful son and useful member of society." Last Will and Testament dated November 29, 1882, witnessed by Judge Jacob Waelder.

9. "A Good Act," San Antonio *Light,* March 6, 1884.

10. Dell Upton, "Defining the Profession: Before 1860," in Joan Ockman, ed. *Architecture School; Three Centuries of Educating Architects in North America* (Washington, D.C.: Association of Collegiate Schools of Architecture) 2012, 39. Upton emphasizes the weight given to the social standing and authority accorded professionals.

11. For a history of the professionalization of architecture in America, see Ockman (2012); Bernard Michael Boyle, "Architectural Practice in America, 1865–1965—Ideal and Reality" in Spiro Kostof, ed., *The Architect: Chapters in the History of the Profession* (New York: Oxford University Press, 1977), 309–344; Andrew Saint, *The Image of the Architect* (New Haven: Yale University Press, 1983); and Cecil D. Elliot, *The American Architect from the Colonial Era to the Present* (Jefferson, North Carolina: McFarland & Co., 2003). The most common reference in the popular literature of the period in question is to say, "so-and-so built this building," which could refer to the designers, carpenters, or clients. Is the builder the one who planned, designed, constructed, paid for, or bought the structure? A Frank Lloyd Wright building is one that he designed, no matter who owns it, in perpetuity. See Tracy Kidder *House* (New York: Houghton Miflin, 1985) for an excellent description of the many justified "builders" and "owners" of a building.

12. Kostof, *The Architect* (1977), v.

13. Richard Upjohn, with whom Kampmann worked on St. Mark's, was a founder and the first president of the AIA from 1857-1876. The Western Association of Architects, based in Chicago since 1884, merged with the AIA in 1889. These organizations fought for national recognition, but most practical matters rested with local chapters. The Texas Society was not founded until 1939. AIA San Antonio is one of seventeen regional chapters in the state.

14. *Memorial and Genealogical Record,* 1894, 658–9.

{ Bibliography }

Historic American Building Surveys [HABS].

National Register of Historic Places.

Newspapers: *Galveston Daily News; San Antonio Light; San Antonio Daily Light; San Antonio Express; San Antonio Daily Express; San Antonio Express News; San Antonio Gazette; San Antonio Herald; San Antonio Evening News; San Antonio Light and Gazette; San Antonio Evening Light*

San Antonio City Directories: 1877-1878; 1891; 1914.

Sanborn Maps, San Antonio, 1885–1954.

Texas State Historic Markers (Texas Historical Commission).

United States Census: 1850, 1860, 1870, 1880, 1890, 1900.

Arreola, Daniel D. "Urban Ethnic Landscape Identity." *Geographical Review* 85 no. 4 (1995): 518–34.

Barnes, Herbert M. "The Course in Architecture at a German 'Technische Hochschule.'" *The American Architect and Building News* 71 (1901): 83–85.

Barnes, Charles Merritt. *Combats and Conquests of Immortal Heroes.* San Antonio: Guessaz & Ferlet, 1910.

Benjamin, Gilbert Giddings. *The Germans in Texas; A Study in Immigration.* New York: Cornell University, 1909.

Bergdoll, Barry. "Ernst Friedrich Zwirner." *Encyclopedia of Architects* 4 (1982): 477–78.

Biesele, Rudolph. *The History of the German Settlements in Texas.* Austin: Von Borkmann–Jones, 1930.

Biographical Encyclopedia of Texas. New York: Southern Publishing Company, 1880.

Booth, John A. and David R. Johnson. The *Politics of San Antonio; Community, Progress, & Power*. Edited by Richard J. Harris. Lincoln: University of Nebraska Press, 1983.

Boryczka, Raymon. "The Busiest Man in Town: John Hermann Kampmann and the Urbanization of San Antonio, Texas, 1884–1885." *Southwestern Historical Quarterly* 115 no. 4 (2012): 329–63.

Boyle, Bernard Michael. *The Architect: Chapters in the History of the Profession*. Edited by Spiro Kostof. New York: Oxford University Press, 1977.

Brain, David. "Practical Knowledge and Occupational Control: The Professionalization of Architecture in the United States." *Sociological Forum* 6 no. 2 (1991): 239–68.

Broadbent, Josephine. "Scrapbook 1905" at the Institute of Texan Cultures.

Carter, James David. *The First Scottish Rite Masonry in Texas, 1867–1967*. Waco: The Scottish Rite Bodies, 1967.

Chabot, Frederick C. *With the Makers of San Antonio: Genealogies of the Early Latin, Anglo-American, and German Families with Occasional Biographies, Each Group Being Prefaced with a Brief Historical Sketch and Illustrations*. San Antonio: Yanaguana Society Publications, 1937.

Chipman, Juanita Herff. Drought The Passing of Gifts. Fort Worth: Xlibris, 2011.

Clark, Mary. "German-English School of San Antonio." *Texas History* 7 (1980).

Corner, William. *San Antonio de Bexar: A Guide and History*. San Antonio: Bainbridge & Corner, 1890.

Cottrell, Debbie Mauldin. "The Country Poor Farm System in Texas." *South West Historical Quarterly* 93 no. 2 (1989): 169–90.

Cox, Wayne. "Archaeological Monitoring for the Casa Rio Restaurant Expansion, San Antonio." *UTSA: Center for Archaeological Research*, 1992.

Cox, Wayne, Anne A. Fox, and Steve A. Tomka. "Archaelogical Background, Museum Reach." *UTSA: Center for Archaeological Research*, 2002.

Crook, Garland E. *San Antonio, Texas 1846–1861*. Rice University: Thesis, 1964.

Custodis, Paul-Georg. *The Church of St. Apollinaris in Remagen, Germany—its Significance and Restoration*. Paris: Icomos, 2002.

Dearen, Patrick. *Halff of Texas: A Merchant Rancher of the Old West*. Fort Worth: Eakin Press, 2000.

Department of Commerce and Labor Bureau of Statistics 33 (1905): 61–62.

Draves, Tim. "Mary Menger (1816–1887)." *The Journal of Life and Culture of San Antonio* (2006).

El-Beheri, Mary Mathis and Susan Clayton. "High School Students Research History of German-English School in San Antonio." *Teaching German* 8 no. 2 (1975): 62–66.

Eliott, Cecil. *The American Architect from the Colonial Era to the Present.* Jefferson: McFarland Press, 2003.

Everett, Donald E. *San Antonio: The Flavor of its Past.* San Antonio: Trinity University, 1975.

Everett, Donald E. *San Antonio's Monte Vista: Architecture and Society in a Gilded Age.* San Antonio: Maverick Publishing, 1999.

Fisher, Lewis F. and Maria Watson Pfeiffer. *San Antonio Architecture: Visions and Traditions.* San Antonio: American Institute of Architects, 2007.

Fisher, Lewis F. *Saint Mark's Episcopal Church: 150 Years of Ministry in Downtown San Antonio.* San Antonio: Maverick Publishing, 2008.

Fisher, Lewis F. *Saving San Antonio: The Precarious Preservation of a Lifetime.* Lubbock: Texas Tech, 1996.

Fox, Anne A. and Marcie Renner. *Historical and Archaeological Investigations at the Site of Rivercenter Mall.* San Antonio: UTSA Center for Archaeological Research, 1999.

Francis Louis des Mazieres Store Building & House, Martinez & South Alamo Streets. San Antonio: Historic American Buildings Survey, 1934.

Geue, Chester W. and Ethel Hander Geue. *A New Land Beckoned: German Immigration to Texas.* San Antonio: Texian Press, 1972.

Geue, Ethel Hander. *New Homes in a New Land: German Immigration to Texas.* Baltimore: Genealogical Pub Co., 1982.

Gold, Theresa. "Charles and Elizabeth Degen." *Our Heritage* 34, no. 4 (1993): 36.

Gold, Theresa. "St. John Celebrates 125 Years in San Antonio." 1993.

Gould, Stephen. *The Alamo City Guide.* New York: Macgowan & Slipper Printers, 1882.

Green, Rena Maverick. *Memoirs of Mary A. Maverick.* San Antonio: Alamo Printing Co., 1921.

Haile, Bartee. "This Week in Texas History." *Lone Star Iconoclast* (2006).

Hagner, Lillie May. *Alluring San Antonio: Through The Eyes of an Artist.* San Antonio: The Naylor Company, 1940.

Hennech, Michael C. and Tracé Etienne-Gray. *Brewing Industry.* San Antonio: Texas Historical Association.

Herff, Eda Kampmann. "Eda Herff's Diary" 1884–86 in possession of Juanita Herff Chipmann.

Herff, Florence Ilse. Ilse's Personal Story in possession of Juanita Herff Chipman.

Heusinger, Edward W. *A Chronology of Events in San Antonio.* San Antonio: 1951.

Hull, Vinton Lee. "Old Times in San Antonio." *Frontier Times* 6 no. 10 (1929).

James, Vinton Lee. *Frontier and Pioneer Recollections of Early Days in San Antonio and West Texas.* San Antonio: 1938.

Jennings, Frank. *San Antonio: Story of an Enchanted City.* San Antonio: San Antonio Express-News, 1998.

Johnson, Frank W. *A History of Texas and Texans Volume III.* San Antonio: American Historical Society, 1914.

Jonus, Jason K. "Major John Herman Kampmann: Leader." *Texas Historical* 49 (1983): 22–29.

Jordan, Terry. "German Houses in Texas." *Landscape* (1964): 24–26.

Jordan, Terry. "German Folk Houses in the Texas Hill Country." *German Culture in Texas* (1980).

Jordan, Terry. "A Gabled Folkhouse of the Mexico/Texas Borderland." (unpublished, ca. 1980).

Jukka Jokilehto History of Architectural Conservation. Butterworth-Heinemann, 2002.

Jutson, Mary Carolyn Hollers. *An English Architect in Texas and Mexico.* San Antonio: Trinity University Press, 1972.

Jutson, Mary Carolyn Hollers. *Biographical Sketch of Alfred Giles.* Finding Aid Alfred Giles Papers, University of Texas, Alexander Architectural Archive.

Keeth, Kent. "Sankt Antonious: Germany in the Alamo City of the 1850s." Southwestern Historical Quarterly 76 (1972): 183–202.

Kesselus, Kenneth. *History of Bastrop County, Texas.* Austin: Jenkins, 1987.

Knight, Lawrence Phillip. *Becoming a City and Becoming American: San Antonio, Texas.* San Antonio: Texas A&M, 1997.

Kostoff, Spiro. *The Architect.* New York: Oxford University Press, 1977.

Kresba, Raymon. *A History of Douglass Academy.* San Antonio: San Antonio Independent School District, 2008.

Lansberry, Homer H. "Menger Hotel Data Pages." Historic American Building Survey, 1936.

Lansberry, Homer H. and Bartlett Cocke. "John W. Kampmann House." Historic American Building Survey, 1937.

Leonard, Chuck. "Visiting Specialist Report on the Bastrop County Courthouse." Comissioned by Texas Historical Commission, 1983.

Lerner, Shirley. *Fire Department History 1848 to 1900.* San Antonio: University of Texas, 1986.

Lich, Glen E. *The German Texans.* San Antonio: Institute of Texas Cultures, 1981.

Long, Christopher. "John M. Fries." Handbook of Texas Online, Texas State Historical Association.

McClintock, William A. "Through Texas and Northern Mexico in 1846–1847." *SHQ* 34, no 2 (1930).

Memorial and Genealogical Record of Southwest Texas. Greenville: Southern Historical Press, 1894.

Mims, Edwin. *A Biography of Sidney Lanier.* Project Gutenberg, 1998.

Moore, Bill. *Bastrop County, 1691–1900.* Bastrop: Bastrop County Historical Society, 1977.

Morganthaler, Jefferson. *The German Settlemant of the Texas Hill Country.* Mockingbird Books, 2007.

Morrison, Andrew. *The City of San Antonio, Texas.* St Louis: Geo Engelhardt, 1890.

Neumann, Ray. *A Centennial History of St. Joseph's Church and Parish.* St. Joseph's, 1968.

Newcomb, Pearson. *Alamo City.* San Antonio: Pearson Newcomb, 1926.

Olmstead, Frederick. *A Journey Through Texas.* London: Sampson Low, Son & Co., 1857.

Ornish, Natalie. *Pioneer Jewish Texans: Their Impact on Texas and American History for Four Hundred Years.* 1989.

Our Heritage 34 no. 3 (1993): 27.

Pease, S. W. *They Came To Texas.* 1940.

Porter, Charles R. Jr. *Spanish Water, Anglo Water; Early Development in San Antonio.* College Station: Texas A&M University Press, 2009.

Proceedings of the City Council Sept. 2 and Dec. 3, 1851 City Clerk's Office, San Antonio.

Ramsdell, Charles. "Old England in Bexar." *San Antonio Express Magazine*, 1948.

Ransdell, Charles. *San Antonio: A Historical and Pictoral Guide*. Austin: University of Texas Press, 1959.

Rapport, Michael. *1848: Year of Revolution*. Basic Books: 2009.

Remy, Caroline. *Study of Transition: San Antonio Frontier to Urban Community 1875–1900*. Trinity University: M.A. Thesis, 1960.

Robinson, Willard. *Gone from Texas: Our Lost Architectural Heritage*. College Station: Texas A&M Press, 1981.

San Antonio American Institute of Architecture Chapter Guide to San Antonio Architecture, 1986.

Santleben, August. *A Texas Pioneer*. New York: Neale Publishing, 1910.

Santos, Sylvia Ann. *Courthouses of Bexar County*. San Antonio: Bexar County Historical Comission, 1979.

Spieser, Adel. *The Story of Theatre in San Antonio*. Thesis: Saint Mary's University, 1948.

Steinfeldt, Cecelia. *San Antonio Was: Seen Through A Magic Lantern*. San Antonio: San Antonio Museum Association, 1978.

Texas Historical Records Survey, Works Progress Administration. Inventory of the County Archives of Texas No. 11, Bastrop County. San Antonio: The Texas Historical Records Survey, 1941.

Tiling, Moritz. *History of the German Element in Texas*. Houston: 1913.

Tucker, Farrell L. "Edifice of Order: San Antonio City Halls and Jails." *Stripes* 39, no. 3 (1999).

Upton, Dell. *Defining the Profession Before 1860*. Washington: Association of Collegiate Schools of Architecture, 2012.

UTSA Center for Archaeological Research Reports.

Wheeler, Kenneth E. *To Wear a City's Crown: The Beginnings of Urban Growth in Texas*. Cambridge: Harvard University Press, 1968.

Williams, Docia Schultz. *The History and Mystery of the Menger Hotel*. Republish of Texas Press, 2000.

Williamson, Roxanne Kuter. *Austin, Texas: An American Architectural History*. San Antonio: Trinity Press, 1973.

Witteman, A. *San Antonio Illustrated in Photo Gravure from Recent Negatives*. New York: The Albertype Co., 1892.

Woods, Mary N. *From Craft to Profession: The Practive of Architecture in Nineteenth Century America.* Berkley: UC, 1999.

Woodford, Sam. "Carry Nation in Texas." *Southwestern Historical Quarterly* 63 (1960): 557–64.

Young, Kevin R. "Edwin Burr Babbitt." *Handbook of Texas Online.* Texas State Historical Association.

Zucker, Paul. "Architectural Education in Nineteenth Century Germany." *The Journal of the Society of Architectural Historians* 2 no. 3 (1942): 6–13.

{ INDEX }

Commerce Street Bridge, 149–50,
150, 151
County Poor House, 157, *157*
Fire Company No. 2, 154–56,
156
General Land Office Building,
Austin, 21–22, *22,* 189*n*10
Rincon School for Colored
Children, *152,* 152–53
San Antonio courthouse and jail
"Bat Cave," 21, 25–27, *26,* 76
Civil War, 91, 98–100, 132
Classical tradition in Germany, 8, 9
Cologne, Germany, 7
Cologne Cathedral, 9, 10–11
Commerce Street Bridge, 149–50,
150, 151
commercial buildings
about, 142
Faltin Store, Comfort, Texas,
142–44, *143*
Kampmann Building/Block, 165,
166–67, 167–68, *169–70*
Kampmann Planing Mill, *117,*
117–20, *118*
Menger Hotel, 82–84, *83,* 86–87,
87
County Poor House, 157, *157,*
204*n*29
Cupples, George, 153

D & A Oppenheimer Bank, 135
Dashiell, Aurelia, 47
Dashiell, J. Y., 47, 51
Dashiell House, 47–51, *48–50,*
193*n*22
Degen, Charles Phillip, 56–58, 82,
194*n*42
Degen, Elizabeth, 57
Degen, Louis, 58
Degen House, 57–58
Degen's Beer, 57–58, 160, 194*n*47

Eagar, Florence, 63
Eagar, Robert, 58–59, 192*n*3
Eagar, Sarah Elizabeth, 46, 58, *62,*
62–63, 194*n*50, 194*n*52
Eagar House, 35, *59–61,* 59–63
Ecclesiological Movement, 96–97
Eichenreht, Marvin, 42, 44
El-Beheri, Ms., 196*n*28
Elgin, J. E., 46
Elmendorf, Emily, 139
entertainment and entertainment
venues, 72–74, 195*n*11
Episcopal mission in San Antonio,
Texas, 91
European politics in mid-1800s,
11–12

F. Groos & Company, 122
Faltin, August, III, 142
Faltin, Friedrich August, 142
Faltin Store, Comfort, Texas, 142–44,
143
Fiesta, San Antonio, 183
Fink, Elizabeth, 57
Fire Company Station No. 2, 154–
56, *156*
Fish, Rev. John F., 91, 198*n*60
Fitzgerald, Mr., 22–24
"A Fog in Santone" (Henry), 150
Ford, O'Neil, 51
Fort Sam Houston, 104
fountain, cast-iron, 113, *114,* 130
Frederick Douglass School, 153,
203*n*13
Freedmen's Bureau, 152
Freethinkers *verein,* 68, 75, 99–100
French Building, 26
Fries, Fred, 19–20
Fries, Johann M. "John"
about, 19–20
Alamo repair, 20
buildings of, 28–29, 191*n*42